Nationalism,
Ethnic Conflict,
and Democracy

A *Journal of Democracy* Book

Nationalism, Ethnic Conflict, and Democracy

Edited by *Larry Diamond*
and Marc F. Plattner

The Johns Hopkins University Press
Baltimore and London

03 02 01 00 99 98 97 96 95 94   5 4 3 2 1

Chapter 8 originally appeared in the *Journal of Democracy*, April 1994; chapters 3-7 and 9 appeared in the October 1993 issue; and chapters 1 and 2 in the October 1992 issue.

The Johns Hopkins University Press
2715 North Charles Street
Baltimore, Maryland 21218-4319
The Johns Hopkins Press Ltd., London

Library of Congress Cataloging-in-Publication Data

Nationalism, ethnic conflict, and democracy / edited by Larry Diamond and Marc F. Plattner.
    p.   cm. — (A Journal of democracy book)
Includes bibliographical references and index.
ISBN 0-8018-5001-0. — ISBN 0-8018-5002-9 (pbk.)
    1. Nationalism. 2. Ethnic relations. 3. Democracy. 4. Nationalism—Case studies.
5. Ethnic relations—Case studies. 6. Democracy—Case studies. I. Diamond, Larry Jay.
II. Plattner, Marc F., 1945- . III. Series
JC311.N323 1994
320.5'4'09045—dc20   94-21022
                                             CIP

A catalog record for this book is available from the British Library.

CONTENTS

ACKNOWLEDGMENTS

This is the third volume drawn from essays in the *Journal of Democracy* to be published as a book by the Johns Hopkins University Press. In this case, we owe a special debt of gratitude to our editor at Johns Hopkins, Henry Tom, who suggested to us that a collection dealing with the issues of nationalism and ethnic conflict would make an especially timely and valuable contribution. As always, it has been a pleasure to work with Henry and his colleagues in both the books and journals divisions at Johns Hopkins.

This volume is built around two seminal essays, "Nationalism and Democracy" by Ghia Nodia and "Democracy in Divided Societies" by Donald L. Horowitz. Nodia presented an earlier version of his essay at a luncheon seminar held at the National Endowment for Democracy in June 1992. Francis Fukuyama was kind enough to serve as a commentator at that seminar, and we thank both him and Shlomo Avineri for agreeing to provide us on short notice with written comments on Nodia's essay for publication in the October 1992 issue of the *Journal*.

Donald L. Horowitz, one of the world's leading authorities on the politics of ethnicity and a member of the *Journal*'s editorial board, both contributed his own essay and helped us to plan a set of three case studies—by Rotimi T. Suberu on Nigeria, Robert L. Hardgrave, Jr., on India, and Hugh Donald Forbes on Canada—which followed his article in the October 1993 issue of the *Journal*. Two related articles—a survey of the situation of minorities in Eastern Europe by Janusz Bugajski and a short and eloquent essay on the dangers of ethnocentric nationalism by Vesna Pešić—appeared along with these four under the heading "The Challenge of Ethnic Conflict." The remaining essay in this collection, on the manipulation of nationalist appeals in Serbia by V.P. Gagnon, Jr., appeared in the April 1994 issue of the *Journal*.

There are many others whom we wish to thank, beginning with the Lynde and Harry Bradley Foundation, which has provided the *Journal* with continuing financial assistance, and the Smith Richardson

Foundation, which has supported an annual editorial internship. The members of our Editorial Board continue to provide invaluable advice and counsel, and our superb staff continues to do a splendid job of transforming manuscripts into published articles. This volume reflects not only the handiwork of our senior editor, Phil Costopoulos, and production editor, Patricia Loo, but the contributions of three successive interns—Kathy Vitz, Kurt Oeler, and Susan M. Brown. We are particularly grateful to Susan for her excellent work in compiling the index.

Finally, we wish to express our thanks once again for the unfailing support given to the *Journal* by the National Endowment for Democracy and especially its president, Carl Gershman. In January 1994, the Endowment's Board of Directors approved not only an expansion in the average length of future issues of the *Journal* but also the establishment of a new International Forum for Democratic Studies built around the *Journal*. The International Forum will include a library and electronic communications network, as well as a regular program of conferences and seminars on significant issues in the study and practice of democracy. We are confident that the establishment of the International Forum will lead to the publication of many more volumes similar to this one.

INTRODUCTION

Larry Diamond and Marc F. Plattner

The past several years have witnessed not only a global resurgence of democracy but also a resurgence of nationalism and of ethnic conflict. It is true, of course, that neither nationalism nor ethnic conflict had disappeared during the preceding decades, but they have unquestionably gained new salience with the decline and fall of European communism. During the Cold War, nationalism had seemed to be on the wane in the industrialized countries. In the First World, nationalist movements like those of the Basques or the Scots appeared as interesting but marginal throwbacks to an earlier era, likely to be overwhelmed by the cosmopolitan and unifying forces that were propelling European integration. And in the Soviet bloc, the imposition of Leninist rule in the name of a universalist ideology kept a lid on nationalist passions.

Thus nationalism had come to be regarded primarily as a phenomenon of the Third World, where its adherents typically adopted the rhetoric of anticolonialism and anti-imperialism. With right-wing nationalism thoroughly discredited by the defeat of the fascist powers in the Second World War, postwar nationalism in the Third World was generally associated with the Left. Accordingly, its supporters and sympathizers often justified it not as an end in itself but as a necessary stage on the way to a more egalitarian and cosmopolitan future. With the downfall of the Soviet Union and the discrediting of communism, however, nationalism has been drifting away from its moorings on the Left; in many of the postcommunist countries it is clearly veering back toward the Right.

Ethnic conflict, too, at least in its more violent manifestations, was viewed as belonging primarily to the Third World. Asia and especially Africa witnessed high levels of ethnic violence throughout the Cold War period. Constitutionally democratic regimes in Sri Lanka, Lebanon, and Nigeria were destroyed or torn apart by ethnic conflict that led to civil war. Elsewhere in Africa, the need to build nations and hold together ethnically plural states was often cited as a justification for the imposition of authoritarian military or one-party rule (as in Kenya and

Indonesia), or for the constriction of civil and political liberties (as in Malaysia and Singapore). Today, with the reemergence of democratic movements in Africa and the attempts to build democracy on the ruins of Soviet and East European communism, ethnic conflict is once again being recognized as a key obstacle to successful democratization.

Ethnic conflict clearly poses a danger to democracy, but the relationship of nationalism to democracy is much more complex. As Ghia Nodia points out in the essay that opens this volume, "Nationalism is a coin with two sides: one is political, the other ethnic." The uneasy relationship between ethnic or prepolitical attachments and civic or political ones can have momentous and explosive human consequences. Serious reflection on this subject quickly leads one to the most fundamental questions about the nature of the political community. The first part of this volume deals with these broader philosophical and historical issues centering around nationalism and its relation to democracy. The remainder of the essays deal on a more practical level with the threats that ethnic passions pose to democracy in what Donald L. Horowitz calls "divided societies."

Nationalism and Democracy

This volume begins with an extraordinary meditation on nationalism and democracy by a young Georgian political thinker named Ghia Nodia, followed by comments on Nodia's essay by two much more well known political theorists, Francis Fukuyama and Shlomo Avineri. Nodia of course recognizes the tensions between nationalism and liberal democracy, but he decisively rejects the increasingly commonplace view that nationalism is simply an enemy of democracy.

It is probably no accident in this respect that Nodia is a Georgian. Though East European democrats may once have regarded nationalism as a useful element in the fight against Soviet domination, today many of them increasingly see it as a threat to democratic consolidation. This view is eloquently advanced in this volume by Vesna Pešić, a leading Serbian democrat who sees the resurgent nationalism in Eastern Europe as ethnocentric and antidemocratic, even neofascist, in its expansionist tendencies and its subordination of individual rights to collective "national" rights. By contrast, democrats from the Caucasus or the Baltics or Central Asia or Ukraine generally continue to view nationalism as an ally of democracy. For in the former Soviet Union, as Nodia notes, "all *real* democratic movements (save the one in Russia proper) were at the same time nationalist."

The central thesis of Nodia's essay is expressed in his contention that "the idea of nationalism is impossible—indeed unthinkable—without the idea of democracy, and that democracy never exists without nationalism. The two are joined in a sort of complicated marriage, unable to live without each other, but coexisting in an almost permanent state of tension." Nodia persuasively argues that the core of democracy is the idea of popular sovereignty—the notion that the will of the people should prevail. Yet there is nothing in democratic theory per se that indicates where the civic or territorial boundaries of the sovereign people should be drawn. There is agreement on the principle of self-determination, but no clear standard for deciding what properly constitutes the "self" that has the right to determine its own political destiny.

The universal character of the modern democratic idea would seem to point to a universal democratic state. (As Francis Fukuyama notes, there is no reason, strictly on the basis of democratic principles, why Canada and the United States should be separate countries.) Yet in fact, democracy has always found its home in particular communities, which in modern times have been generated principally by nationalism. The nation, as Nodia puts it, "is another name for 'We the People.'"

This does not mean that Nodia accepts the older nationalist view that there are rational or objectively valid criteria on the basis of which the world can be divided up into different national communities, or that the nation is a universal feature of human life. He follows such prominent scholars of nationalism as Hans Kohn, Ernest Gellner, Elie Kedourie, and Anthony D. Smith in regarding nationalism not as a primordial phenomenon but as one born around the time of the French and Industrial Revolutions—a view in which both Fukuyama and Avineri emphatically concur.[1] But the fact that the nation is an "artificial construct" created in part by the human imagination does not, Nodia argues, make it any less essential for providing the political cohesion necessary for a self-governing modern state.

Prior to the eighteenth century, democracy was considered a form of political rule sustainable only in very small territories; some form of monarchy was regarded as inevitable in larger political units. Only in a state essentially limited to a single city could citizens truly know one another and have the communal spirit needed for self-government. This is an argument strongly reiterated by Jean-Jacques Rousseau, the great eighteenth-century proponent of the sovereignty of the people, who was himself born a citizen of the city-state of Geneva. In the "Dedication to the Republic of Geneva" that precedes his *Discourse on Inequality*, Rousseau praises the land of his birth as "a society limited by the extent of human faculties—that is, limited by the possibility of being well-governed . . . where that sweet habit of seeing and knowing one another turned love of the fatherland into love of the citizens rather than love of the soil."[2] Yet Rousseau is also regarded as the thinker who prepared the modern basis of "the identification of nation and state" and who provided "the theoretical foundations upon which alone the nationalism of the nineteenth century could be built."[3]

There is a paradox here. If nationalism is, as Ernest Gellner plausibly defines it, "a political principle which holds that the political and the national unit should be congruent," then a champion of the city-state cannot be a nationalist.[4] Citizens of ancient Athens or Sparta owed their primary political allegiance to their city, not to the Greek nation. A citizen of Geneva was only secondarily a Swiss or a Francophone. If self-government requires that the basic political unit be much smaller than the nation, then nationalism is incompatible with democracy.

This paradox is confronted if not resolved by Rousseau in *Considerations on the Government of Poland* (1772). This is plainly his most "nationalistic" work, filled with passages like the following:

> An infant upon opening his eyes ought to see the fatherland (*patrie*) and until his death should see nothing else. Every true republican imbibes with his mother's milk the love of the fatherland, that is, of the laws and of liberty. This love constitutes his entire existence; he sees nothing but the fatherland, and lives for it alone; the moment he is by himself, he is nothing; the moment he no longer has a fatherland, he is no more, and if he is not dead, he is worse than dead.[5]

Yet in a chapter entitled "The Radical Vice," Rousseau cites the "largeness of nations" as the principal source of human misfortunes, and questions whether successful political reform is even possible for a nation as big as Poland.[6] He goes on to advocate a decentralized federal system, but makes it clear that the federal units must remain subordinate to "the body of the Republic" and that all the citizens must be devoted first and foremost to Poland. In practical terms, then, Rousseau acknowledges the hope of reforming and democratizing large states.[7]

Rousseau's passionate advocacy of popular sovereignty and of republican self-government clearly has taken root in the modern world, while the small city-state has been consigned to a past that seems irretrievably lost. But how can one achieve in a large modern state the kind of political cohesiveness needed for popular self-rule? The answer that Rousseau reluctantly adopts in his advice to the Poles—and that was more enthusiastically taken up by his disciples during the French Revolution—is *nationalism*. The passive subjects of a king or emperor or dictator may include many different peoples who acknowledge no other common bond. But citizens who are expected to fight and to die for their country must come to consider themselves as part of one people, even if they live vast distances from one another and never meet once in their lives. For this reason, nationalism in some form would seem to be a necessary accompaniment to popular self-government and thus to modern democracy.

As Nodia emphasizes, however, popular sovereignty is only one aspect of modern *liberal* democracy, and it is the relationship of nationalism to liberalism that is especially problematic (as Pešić also asserts). Yet, while acknowledging that there is a serious tension between liberalism, which exalts the freedom to choose of the individual, and nationalism, which emphasizes a collective identity that normally is not a matter of individual choice, Nodia argues that there is also an underlying kinship. He finds this link in (as Avineri puts it) "the Kantian doctrine of human personality and autonomy," which Nodia sees as supplying the basis for the concept of self-determination (i.e., obeying only laws that have been self-imposed) on which nationalism is founded. Pursuing this line of argument, he contends that just as individuals require other individuals for mutual recognition, so do nations need other nations. "The idea of nationhood," he concludes, "is an idea of membership in humanity, and the idea of humanity as a 'family of nations' has long been a mainstay of liberal nationalism." He thus invokes a nationalism of the kind envisaged in the United Nations Charter, where each nation finds its place in the sun of international recognition and does not seek to overshadow its fellow nations.

Nodia realizes, of course, that the real world is a long way from this point, and that the ugly chauvinistic and illiberal aspects of nationalism are far from tamed, especially in the postcommunist world. Nor is he optimistic that the problems posed by interethnic relations in Eastern Europe and the former Soviet Union can be solved without great pain and bloodshed. Nonetheless, he holds that these problems cannot be alleviated by wishing away the power of nationalism, the only effective unifying force in the atomized societies left behind by the demise of totalitarianism. Thus he concludes:

> The best available counterbalance to the nationalism that lives in the past and fixates on old grievances and old ambitions is an alternative version of the nationalist sentiment that makes it a point of national honor to join the civilized world as an equal and dignified member.

Although they might agree on little else, Francis Fukuyama and Shlomo Avineri are united in their praise of Nodia's essay and in support of the view that moderate nationalism can be an ally of democracy. Expressing his basic concurrence with Nodia's "vindication of nationalism in the context of modernity," Avineri emphasizes that the depreciation of nationalism as provincial and retrograde is in large part a product of "the cultural imperialism of Great Nations." Large peoples like the English, the French, and the Russians, he argues, have unthinkingly and mistakenly regarded their own cultures as the very hallmark of advanced civilization, and thus have consistently been blinded to the strength of nationalist aspirations on the part of smaller peoples. This is especially true with regard to the nations of the East, which are reentering history after decades of communist repression and

must now seek to work out their own reconciliations of nationalism with
liberal democracy.

Fukuyama, despite endorsing significant parts of Nodia's argument,
also raises some major points of disagreement, especially on the
fundamental question of the ultimate compatibility of nationalism and
liberalism. Fukuyama is willing to grant the utility—perhaps even the
necessity—of nationalism as a "transitional strategy" for getting to liberal
democracy, particularly in the postcommunist world. He also concedes
that a "tolerant" nationalism (i.e., one in which "national identity is
pushed off into the realm of private life and culture, rather than being
politicized and made the basis of legal rights") can coexist reasonably
well with liberalism. Yet he cautions that such coexistence works best
either in relatively homogeneous countries like Japan or France, where
the dominant culture is secure, or in "lands of new settlement" like the
United States or Australia, where the dominant culture is less ethnically
based.

But if the national principle is admitted into the political realm,
Fukuyama argues, "Persons who do not belong to the dominant
nationality *ipso facto* have their dignity recognized in an inferior way
to those who do belong—a flat contradiction of the principle of
universal and equal recognition" (which he sees as the very heart of
liberalism). Thus Fukuyama fears that in the postcommunist East, where
most states are "rough ethnic patchworks," the problem of the rights of
ethnic minorities will pose a continuing threat to the consolidation of
liberal democracy. As for a solution based on the principle of group
rights, he points to the sad experience of Lebanon as an example of the
terrible practical difficulties that this entails, and concludes that the only
secure basis for liberal democracy is the Kantian principle that
recognizes people as individual human beings rather than as members
of particular national groups.

The Challenge of Ethnic Conflict

Running through all of the essays in this collection is a common
concern with a fundamental dilemma of the modern nation-state, to
which we have alluded above: How can particularistic and often
antagonistic group identities be reconciled with the unifying mission of
the modern state? More especially, how can this be done in a
democratic state?

Political theorists and actors have responded to this question with
widely different strategies. Many have contended, often with the support
of passionate and broad nationalist movements, that every national
people should have a state of its own. In the nineteenth century, this led
to the great European state-building and nation-building projects,
particularly in Bismarck's Germany and Cavour's Italy, where various

principalities and autonomous polities were forged into a common whole united by language and some sense of shared origin, experience, and culture.

A second strategy has been not to bring people together but to break them apart through secession of one group from a state or empire dominated by some "other" people. Here, the political leaders of an aggrieved people have sought to establish coincidence between nation and state by reducing the size of the state to fit the particular nation, thus giving territory and sovereignty to what had previously been an oppressed ethnic minority. This strategy has enjoyed international legitimacy ever since Woodrow Wilson took the United States into the First World War in part to defend the principle of self-determination, and especially since it was written into the very first article (Section 2) of the United Nations Charter. Throughout this century, "self-determination" has been the international justification not only for anticolonial movements but for the struggles of minority peoples everywhere seeking a state of their own: the Armenians, the Kurds, the Kashmiris, the Igbos, the Eritreans, the Katangans, the Sri Lankan Tamils, the Philippine Moros, the Karen of Burma, the Southern Sudanese, the Basques, the Québécois. (Irredentist movements by minority peoples in one state to join politically with ethnic kin who predominate in a neighboring state form a subtype of this tendency.) Though frozen by half a century of communist rule, such secessionist and irredentist pressures have a long history in Eastern Europe, which is now being revived by what Janusz Bugajski calls in this volume "a far-reaching ethnic reawakening" in the region.

Secession as an approach to solving the dilemma of state and nation typically only raises further problems, however. For the region seeking "self-determination" typically harbors its own minority groups and, not infrequently, multiple ethnic or nationalist movements with different conceptions of what constitutes "the nation" and what are the boundaries that should circumscribe the state. Even within the same ethnic group there often coexist quite different political conceptions of the desirability of secession.[8] By what process—and, if electorally, by what percentage of the vote—should "self-determination" take place? And if, as is almost always the case, the agitants for secession contain within their claimed territory actual or would-be minorities of their own, what rights do these minorities have? If the "primary" minority can secede from the state, may not the "secondary" minorities secede from the "primary" minority? Here again we confront the dilemma we noted above with respect to nationalism. As Sir W. Ivor Jennings once noted, "the people cannot decide until somebody decides who are the people." As the creation of Pakistan and then its 1971 dismemberment attest, subethnic or subnational cleavages may increase sharply in salience once a larger cleavage is removed through the redefinition of state boundaries. The problem of learning to manage and process diversity does not disappear, but only recedes to a different level.

In their anticolonial struggles and postindependence political endeavors, Asian, African, and Middle Eastern political leaders followed a third strategy of state-building and nation-building. In striving to mute cultural differences or merge them into a broader, overarching political identity owing allegiance to a strong, centralized state, their efforts in many ways paralleled (and were modeled on) the Italian, German, and other European success stories. Although this strategy yielded success when different peoples coalesced in opposition to a common European colonial oppressor, postindependence "nation-building" projects in the Third World often failed miserably, particularly in Africa. India was a stunning exception, uniting more than 500 princely states with the former British territory and overcoming severe linguistic divisions—but not without first experiencing the bloody trauma of partition. In most cases, decolonization produced new states whose boundaries had been drawn artificially for the political purposes of the colonizers, and not (as in Europe) forged through a more organic political (even if at times also coercive) process of unification. Worse still, the objective obstacles to the emergence of a common sense of nationhood were considerably greater than in nineteenth-century Europe, given the tremendous linguistic and cultural diversity contained within the new states. Many of the postcolonial states were composed of groups with radically different political and cultural traditions, and even histories of mutual hatreds for one another. Moreover, these states had virtually none of the financial, industrial, military, and technological resources of Bismarckian Germany or even Czarist Russia.

Poor in resources, institutionally shallow, internationally dependent, politically insecure, and ethnically riven, the new states of Africa and much of Asia failed both at state-building and at nation-building. The result was not only chronic political instability and repression (carried out by leaders desperate to hang on to power and by dominant groups anxious to preserve their hegemony) but also ethnic rioting, conflict, and civil war. A conservative estimate would count at least half the states of Sub-Saharan Africa—including Angola, Mozambique, Rwanda, Burundi, Zaire, Uganda, Ethiopia, Somalia, Sudan, Chad, Nigeria, Liberia, Zimbabwe, and South Africa—have experienced since their independence either civil war or deaths in the thousands from violence based on ethnic or racial divisions.

The human toll of these and other political failures has been horrendous: half a million deaths and eleven million refugees from the 1947 partition of the Indian subcontinent; an estimated one million deaths during the Nigerian civil war (1967-70); several hundred thousand deaths during the ethnic and political terror of Idi Amin (1971-79) and Milton Obote (1981-85) in Uganda; tens of thousands of deaths and

600,000 persons displaced during a decade of ongoing civil war in Sri Lanka; more than two hundred thousand deaths and an estimated 2.5 million refugees as a result of wars in the former Yugoslavia; well over a hundred thousand deaths and half a million refugees from the eruption of fighting in Rwanda between the majority Hutu and the once feudally dominant but minority Tutsi in 1994. Even where federal institutions keep more localized conflicts from spreading, they can impose a large human toll, as shown by the 20,000 deaths in Punjab and 12,000 in Kashmir since those separatist struggles against India exploded into open insurgency during the 1980s. Probably well over a million people have died from ethnic conflict in the two decades since Harold Isaacs estimated that ethnic violence had claimed more than ten million lives since the Second World War.[9]

Clearly, the costs associated with failed states and riven nations are enormous. With the end of the Cold War, the retreat of ideology, and the resurgence of competing ethnic and nationalist identities, the problem of ethnic conflict has never been more urgent.

Divided Societies

In assembling the articles included in the second part of this volume, we sought answers to several questions: What are the sources of ethnic identity and conflict, and why has ethnic pluralism been so difficult to reconcile with democracy? What accounts for the eruption of ethnic pluralism into destructive violence in some countries, and its relatively peaceful management in other countries, or at other times in the same countries? To what extent have the constitution, electoral system, and devolution of power been explicitly designed to mitigate ethnic conflict, and how have they affected the salience of ethnic conflict in party politics, government, and social life? What lessons can be learned—from both successes and failures—about how to control ethnic conflict within a democratic state? In short, can ethnic pluralism and democracy be reconciled? If so, how?

In "Democracy in Divided Societies," which builds on his seminal work, *Ethnic Groups in Conflict*, Donald L. Horowitz explains why "severely divided societies" represent a particularly serious threat to democratic polities. Some conceptual clarification is in order here. We use *ethnicity* in this volume to refer to a highly inclusive (and relatively large-scale) group identity based on some notion of common origin, recruited primarily through kinship, and typically manifesting some measure of cultural distinctiveness. "So conceived, ethnicity easily embraces groups differentiated by color, language, and religion; it covers 'tribes,' 'races,' 'nationalities,' and castes."[10] Although ascriptive in nature, ethnicity is not entirely immutable (even though it may appear so in particular conflictual situations): group boundaries may shift as groups divide, merge, erode, aggregate, and redefine themselves over time (in part by recasting or reinventing myths of common origin). Occasionally, when ethnic boundaries are not maintained by clear physical markings, individuals may cross ethnic lines. In some ethnically plural societies, ethnicity may have only modest salience, as one among several identities an individual may possess. Ethnic boundaries may be fluid and may be heavily eroded over time through intermarriage (as Horowitz notes has happened between the Thais and Chinese in Thailand or the Taiwanese and Mainlanders in Taiwan). In other deeply divided societies, ethnic cleavages have proved particularly rigid and enduring. It is these societies—located primarily in Africa, Asia (including the former Soviet Central Asia), the Middle East, and (especially Eastern) Europe—that are the primary concern of this book.

For several reasons, ethnicity is the most difficult type of cleavage for a democracy to manage. Because ethnicity taps cultural and symbolic issues—basic notions of identity and the self, of individual and group worth and entitlement—the conflicts it generates are intrinsically less amenable to compromise than those revolving around material issues. When the struggle is over money, taxes, wage levels, business regulations, social welfare, infrastructural investments, or similar issues, the gains and losses are divisible in a variety of ways. "In growing economies, especially, a wide range of solutions may be available for constructive bargainers."[11] Ethnic conflicts often involve such material issues and may sometimes be resolved through conventional kinds of bargaining. But because at bottom they revolve around exclusive symbols and conceptions of legitimacy, they are characterized by competing demands that cannot easily be broken down into bargainable increments. For example, "How does a policymaker divide up the 'glorification' of the national language?"[12] The political status of a group's language is an enormously sensitive issue—as Hugh Donald Forbes shows here in his case study of officially bilingual Canada—because it symbolizes the relative worth and legitimacy of a group in the system. It can also become a powerful tool of political domination and material advantage.[13] Ethnic cleavages become even more volatile when competing notions of morality—of the sacred and the profane—are invoked, as in religious conflict. Thus did the dispute over the Ayodhya mosque, and its eventual destruction by Hindu-fundamentalist mobs in 1992, trigger furious religious rioting that claimed over a thousand lives across India.

In deeply divided societies, ethnicity—in contrast to other lines of cleavage, such as class or occupation—appears permanent and all-encompassing, predetermining who will be granted and denied access to power and resources. In such a context, "floating voters" are largely absent. Democratic elections take on the character of a "census" and constitute a zero-sum game: one ethnic group or coalition or party wins by its sheer demographic weight, and others see themselves as losing all, excluded not only from the government but also from the larger political community.[14] The fear that this exclusion may be permanent is not unreasonable. As Horowitz demonstrates, the historical record is replete with cases in which a particular ethnic group or narrow coalition—often a distinct minority of the total population—firmly entrenched its control over the state once it had achieved power, by whatever means.

For all these reasons, many scholars have expressed profound skepticism about the possibility of stable democracy in societies in which ethnicity has become politicized. Examining the wave of African and Asian democratic failures during the 1950s and 1960s, Alvin Rabushka and Kenneth Shepsle concluded that "democracy . . . is simply not viable in an environment of intense ethnic preferences." In what they termed "plural societies" (essentially, deeply divided ones), where ethnic differences are sharpened through cohesive political organization, multiethnic coalitions inevitably break down, brokerage institutions disappear, all distributive (not to mention cultural) issues are reflected through the prism of ethnicity, and ethnic moderation becomes untenable.[15] A number of comparative and statistical analyses have seemed to confirm this pessimism.[16] G. Bingham Powell's innovative study of contemporary democracies added another empirical dimension of explanation: Countries with extreme ethnic complexity experience high levels of deadly political violence, which severely strains the fabric of their democratic orders.[17]

More than other forms of government, democracy, as a system of institutionalized competition and conflict, requires reliable means for managing conflict peacefully and constitutionally, keeping it within certain boundaries of decency, order, and restraint. Robert Dahl emphasizes the importance of accommodative elite practices and understandings in evolving a system of "mutual security" that ensures some minimal level of protection for the basic interests of every major political competitor, such that defeat will not mean total or permanent exclusion from power and resources.[18] Such a deeply rooted sense of mutual trust among political competitors is vital to securing another condition for stable democracy: tolerance of opposition. Forbes shows how important the early historical emergence of elite accommodation and tolerance (facilitated by a small state and a rough and stable balance of forces in the country) has been to the management of conflict between English and French Canadians.

Once deep ethnic divisions are mobilized into electoral and party politics, however, they tend to produce suspicion rather than trust, acrimony rather than civility, polarization rather than accommodation, and victimization rather than toleration. Amidst such conditions, and the consequent fear of subversion on the part of an ethnically based ruling party whose opposition hates it and feels no stake in the process, the appeal to a larger nationalism coincident with the state "does not so much encourage toleration of dissent and opposition as . . . [provide] a ready and acceptable justification for intolerance and repression."[19] As V.P. Gagnon shows in the case of Serbia, it is not only other ethnic groups who are at risk of such repression, but moderates from the dominant group whose calls for accommodation can leave them open to denunciation as "traitors" to the national cause. Mutual suspicion is especially likely, Bugajski notes, where (as in much of Eastern Europe) minority peoples have ethnic kin who dominate in a neighboring state, and are backed politically by them. Horowitz captures this problem well in his contribution to this volume:

> An ethnically differentiated opposition can easily be depicted as consisting of particularly dangerous enemies: historical enemies, enemies who do not accept the current identity of the state, enemies who are plotting to break up the state or to steal it for their own group—as indeed they may be, given the crucial importance of state power and the costs of exclusion from it.

Such depictions lead naturally to the imposition of increasingly authoritarian measures and ultimately a one-party state, which, as Horowitz rightly notes here, has been "a mask for ethnic domination" in Africa.

Another means by which democracies manage, soften, complicate, and contain conflict is through the generation of cross-cutting cleavages. When people who are divided along one line of cleavage, such as religion, interact and find common ground with one another along a different line of cleavage, such as class, they experience psychological "cross-pressures" that tend to moderate their political views and induce them generally toward greater tolerance and accommodation.[20] Although the positive effects of such phenomena are readily apparent in modern, industrialized democracies like Canada or the United States, they are little in evidence in the deeply divided societies of Africa and Asia. This is explained only in part by the fact that these societies are much less developed economically and therefore manifest much less class and occupational complexity that could generate other interests to cross-cut ethnicity. Two other features of ethnicity itself also come into play. First, in deeply divided societies ethnic allegiances are all-encompassing, seeping into "organizations, activities, and roles to which they are formally unrelated. The permeative character of ethnic affiliations, by infusing so many sectors of social life, imparts a pervasive quality to ethnic conflict and raises sharply the stakes of ethnic politics."[21] Second, in many deeply divided societies other objective lines of cleavage cumulate with ethnicity rather than cross-cut it, so some ethnic groups are distinctly richer, better educated, and more advanced in industry and commerce than others. The more prosperous groups (or sometimes the less prosperous ones) may have a lockhold on political power owing to their greater numbers, or on the military (and thus political power) owing to colonial design or some other accident of history.

Sifting through a wealth of recent data, Horowitz highlights other reasons why severely divided societies do not easily give rise to or maintain democracy. Ethnic minorities may tolerate authoritarian or semi-authoritarian regimes out of the knowledge (and historical memory) that their political treatment could be much worse. Elsewhere, historical memories intrude viciously to offer competing exclusive conceptions of community and territorial legitimacy. To Horowitz's examples of this phenomenon one could add the Hindu-Moslem conflict over the Ayodhya mosque, as Robert Hardgrave discusses in his chapter on India, or the Arab-Israeli conflict over Jerusalem, Hebron, or Israel itself. Their ethnic antagonists assert that Jews do not belong in Palestine; nor Hungarians in Romania; nor Tamils in Sri Lanka; nor whites in South Africa. In each case, the message from the group that claims a greater territorial legitimacy is: Go Home. When leaders of the majority group(s) find it to their political advantage, they may (officially or not) mobilize violence to pursue strategies of expulsion, "ethnic cleansing," or, ultimately, genocide. The cynical campaign of President Daniel arap Moi's regime in Kenya, narrowly based in the Kalenjin ethnic group, to drive Kikuyu settlers from the Rift Valley through terror and violence is just one lesser-known example of a disturbingly common contemporary phenomenon. By late 1993, Human Rights Watch estimates, 1,500 Kenyans had been killed and 300,000 displaced in these "tribal clashes."[22] Prospects for democracy in Kenya have been another (quite deliberate) casualty.

One of the striking themes that runs through our case studies of ethnic conflict is the extent to which politicians mobilize it for their own immediate political advantage. In Nigeria, this political opportunism can be seen particularly in the dynamics leading to the breakdown of the First Republic and the onset of the civil war, but it has been a recurrent feature of electoral politics. In India, it has played a major role in the intensification and politicization of religious conflict between Hindus and Muslims. As Susanne and Lloyd Rudolph have argued, that conflict is not a new eruption of "ancient hatreds" but the creation of present-day militant politicians and intellectuals, springing not from the disadvantaged but from the elite, who thought they could ride to power by "hijack[ing] Hinduism—replacing its diversity . . . with a monotheistic Ram cult."[23]

In this volume, V.P. Gagnon, Jr., advances a similar thesis to explain the origins of nationalist war and aggression in the former Yugoslavia. Serbia's violent conflicts with Croatia and then Bosnia began not from "the spontaneous eruption of 'ancient ethnic hatreds,' brewing in a

cultural and historical context hostile to democratization," not even from
an objective conflict of interest between these nationalities, but rather as
"part of a purposeful and rational strategy planned and carried out by
the minority of actors in Serbia who were most threatened by
democratizing and liberalizing currents within the Serbian Communist
party." Those actors—namely, Slobodan Milošević and his hard-line
communist allies—skillfully created and manipulated images of a threat
to the Serbian people and feelings of ethnic hatred, in order to
overwhelm their democratic opponents (and some notable inclinations
toward interethnic harmony at the mass level) in a wave of nationalist
reaction. This Serbian tragedy reflects, Vesna Pešić argues in her brief
essay, a regional pattern in which old communist elites have "used
national feelings and fears to serve their own ambitions."

If this analytic perspective is profoundly discouraging in revealing the
scope of human tragedy that can result from greed for power and
irresponsible leadership, it is, strangely, also hopeful in its implications.
For if ethnic conflict and nationalist aggression originate more from the
rational (albeit utterly unscrupulous) pursuit of political opportunities and
incentives than from visceral and immutable passions, they can,
presumably, also be contained by the restructuring of incentives.

An important message of Horowitz's scholarly work is that
demography is not destiny. The presence of even severe ethnic divisions
need not condemn a country to ethnic violence and instability if it
adopts political institutions that offer incentives for accommodation rather
than polarization. The party system, as Horowitz observes here, may
perform this service more naturally if it has developed in such a way
as to emphasize other cleavages. Canadian democracy was fortunate to
have had from the beginning multiethnic "brokerage" parties that fed off
of internal divisions within the English and French communities and
bridged the cultural divide between them. But such cross-cutting parties
have spontaneously emerged mainly in older polities in which ethnicity
rose to salience after other lines of cleavage, such as class and religion,
shaped partisan alignments. In emerging democracies, deliberate
constitutional engineering is a vital tool of ethnic conflict management.
Yet, as Horowitz notes in concluding his contribution to this volume,
timing is crucial. As the tragedy in the former Yugoslavia most
poignantly illustrates, once the dynamics of violent conflict take over,
hatred, fear, and vengeance—however "modern"—may overwhelm
rationality.

Reducing Ethnic Conflict in Democracies

Horowitz's own theoretical essay and the country studies in this
volume attest to the complexity and diversity of ethnic conflict and thus
the inappropriateness of any single formula for conflict management.

Nevertheless, there are some broad lessons to be learned, and some specific institutional arrangements worth noting.

The most general lesson, eloquently elucidated by Horowitz and by Rotimi Suberu in his case study of Nigeria, is the paramount need to avoid the indefinite and complete exclusion from political power of particular groups, whether majority or minority. All groups must be given some stake in the system. And no minority should be allowed to establish a permanent political hegemony at the center; power should be open to rotation.[24] Various constitutional and electoral arrangements may help to ensure this, depending on the circumstances. One lesson that clearly emerges from Bugajski's review of the fate of minorities in Eastern Europe is the importance of meaningful and constitutionally entrenched provisions for minority rights, including "guarantees of nondiscrimination on ethnic, religious, or racial grounds, as well as the opportunity to express and develop minority cultures and languages" (in part through private schools). In return, Bugajski argues, minority leaders must recognize their obligation to affirm the legitimacy and territorial integrity of the state.

In numerous writings over the past two decades, Arend Lijphart has proposed a "consociational" formula to manage the ethnic cleavages of deeply divided societies. This involves power-sharing arrangements with four key features: grand coalitions at the center, minority veto powers, federalism (where ethnic cleavages are territorially based) to provide some autonomy for groups to manage their own affairs, and proportionality in the distribution of legislative seats, government posts, and public funds.[25] Most serious students of ethnic conflict acknowledge the importance of federalism, or some substantial devolution of power, as an instrument for what Horowitz calls "democratic remediation." In addition, many, including Horowitz, recognize the value of non-plurality electoral systems as an instrument to help secure group interests and induce moderation. However, Horowitz sees the consociational model as seriously flawed in two respects. First, he views grand, all-inclusive governing coalitions as inherently unsustainable amidst the political tensions and jealousies of deep ethnic divisions. Second, he sees consociational formulas as least useful precisely in the most intensely conflictual circumstances, where there do not yet exist elite traditions of and motivations for accommodation (an important precondition of the Lijphart model and its success in European countries like the Netherlands).

The key, Horowitz argues, is to design political institutions so as to "make moderation pay," even for leaders who have no intrinsic inclination toward it.[26] Hope lies, he believes, in the emergence of more limited but nevertheless truly multiethnic political coalitions that will bring multiple groups into political power and keep them mutually dependent on one another. If such coalitions are too broad, however, they could become unwieldy and unsustainable (as the Zambian Movement for Multiparty Democracy has proven to be), because there are insufficient resources to distribute to everyone.

The ideal arrangement, Horowitz implies, may be a system of competing multiethnic coalitions that alternate in power over time. Unfortunately, his primary example of such a system, in the Indian state of Kerala, emerged out of idiosyncratic circumstances, and it is doubtful that constitutional engineers, merely by the force of their rules, could replicate it. And even if such a system does develop, it is not immune to serious erosion over time: Witness the tremendous recent volatility in Canada's party system, which, in the November 1993 parliamentary elections (shortly after the original publication of Forbes's article), virtually eliminated one of the two key bridging parties, the Progressive Conservatives, while giving large numbers of seats to two regionalist parties, the Bloc Québécois and the Western-based Reform Party.

Nevertheless, some glimmers of hope may be found in the recent Nigerian experience, notwithstanding the tragic abortion of democracy via the country's third military coup against a civilian regime on 17 November 1993, after Suberu's article was first published in the *Journal*. Of course, the Nigerian example has many negative aspects: Politics and governance continue to be disfigured by appalling levels of political corruption on the part of both civilians and military officers.[27] The two political parties created by the military were artificial in nature and fractured along various ethnic and factional lines, and each had certain ethnic or regional centers of gravity. Yet both parties won state governorships in various parts of the country, established national support bases, and represented true multiethnic coalitions with the capacity for alternating in power over time. Both, Suberu shows, ensured broad ethnic balance in their respective leadership structures through the practice of "zoning" various offices to different ethnic or regional constituencies. Moreover, the two parties did draw upon more spontaneous and organic trends of political convergence that had been under way at the end of the Second Republic in 1983 (and in some respects dated back to the First Republic of the 1960s), and something like those two multiethnic coalitions probably would have emerged in any case even if the military had not mandated them.[28]

Further promise for Nigeria can be inferred from the results of the June 1993 presidential election, which was annulled by a military regime that did not truly want to surrender power. In that election, a southerner, Moshood Abiola, was elected president for the first time, winning several northern states (including his opponent's home state of Kano) and a substantial share of the Igbo vote even though his opponent had an Igbo vice-presidential running mate while Abiola did not. This was a natural progression from the logic of national presidential politics during the Second Republic, when a provision requiring a broad distribution of regional support for a candidate to be elected president provided a major incentive to transethnic political appeals and coalitions.[29] As Horowitz observed in his earlier work, however, promising electoral incentives like this one can be offset or overcome by the contradictory pull of other variables, including other features of the political and electoral systems. It is unfortunate, as Suberu emphasizes, that the proliferation of states in Nigeria (which Horowitz had cited in 1985 as an obstacle to the consolidation of a broad, multiethnic party system) continued under the cynical military rule of General Ibrahim Babangida, who increased the number of states from 19 to 30, doubled the number of local government areas, and whetted local appetites for further fragmentation while centralizing the exercise of real political power. It is also unfortunate (as Suberu notes) that the drafters of the 1989 Nigerian constitution did not consider alternative methods for conducting legislative elections. A different electoral system, one that encourages people to pool votes across ethnic lines, might have better represented dissident sentiments and subethnic cleavages within various ethnic strongholds.

The military's annulment of Nigeria's 1993 presidential election was tragic not merely because of the broad multiethnic character of Abiola's victory but also on account of his capacity, as a Yoruba Muslim from the predominantly Christian southern half of the country, to reverse what Suberu identifies as an ominous and growing religious polarization in the country. This capacity was due in part to the historically moderate and bridging role on religious issues of the Yoruba, a people who straddle the Christian-Muslim divide to a degree that no other major ethnic group even approaches; and in part to Abiola's own political inclination toward moderation, pragmatism, and interethnic coalition-building. Suberu's chapter points both to the potential danger of religion as a polarizing cleavage, bifurcating the polity in a way that the more complex ethnic cleavage does not, and to the importance of politically responsible leadership that eschews the mobilization of religious issues for short-term political gains. Both points are emphasized as well in Hardgrave's case study of India.

All three of our country case studies underscore, as Horowitz's theoretical and comparative work has done, the enormous potential value of federalism as a tool for managing, containing, and reducing ethnic conflict. Federalism is pivotal, Horowitz has argued, because it can perform any or all of five functions to reduce ethnic conflict. Usually it *disperses conflict*, "by proliferating the points of power so as to take the heat off a single focal point."[30] Dispersal of conflict, Hardgrave concludes, has been a prominent effect of federalism in India, "compartmentaliz[ing] friction" in such a way that "[t]he cultural conflicts of one state rarely spill over into another," thus better enabling the center to "manage and contain them." Depending on how the boundaries of the states or regions are drawn, federalism may *generate intraethnic conflict* by activating subgroup identities with the devolution of power (as has occurred in both India and Nigeria). It may create incentives and opportunities for *interethnic cooperation*, for example by creating ethnically heterogeneous states (as in Malaysia) in which different groups must coalesce to gain advantage from the center. It may encourage *alignments on nonethnic interests*, as occurred in Nigeria when some of the newly created states (cutting across ethnic divisions) found themselves with oil, and others without, some with substantial infrastructure, and others with little. Finally, through redistribution from the center to state and even local governments, federalism may *reduce material disparities* among ethnic groups.[31] In addition, decentralization permits groups that may have no hope of being prominent in the central government to have some "venue to express their cultural distinctiveness" (to quote Hardgrave), some control over their own affairs, and some resources to apply toward them. Such devolution of power has proven essential for avoiding the political alienation and embitterment of significant minority groups in Nigeria and India, as well as Canada and Spain; it is clearly necessary for stability and peace in Eastern Europe and will be vital to the future of a democratic South Africa.

It matters greatly, however, how federalism is structured and implemented. One critical issue is whether to create homogeneous or heterogeneous subfederal units. By reorganizing state boundaries along linguistic lines within a decade of independence, Hardgrave argues, India enhanced the sense of cultural security of major ethnic groups and facilitated greater political participation, albeit at the cost of reinforcing prejudice against nonindigenes. This negative effect has been a growing problem in Nigeria as well, and underscores the difficult trade-offs involved in the structuring of a federal system.

A second key issue is the number of subfederal units. When states proliferate endlessly, no federal system can develop the institutional maturity and stable expectations it needs to function effectively. Moreover, "the strategy of dicing the country up into smaller and increasingly unviable states and localities" generates fiscal strains and bureaucratic waste, while actually shifting power back to the center. This major insight of Suberu's case study of Nigeria is confirmed by Horowitz's comparative work (as well as Hardgrave's detailing of India's relative prudence and restraint in creating additional states). Since Nigeria's territorial fragmentation has not, Suberu shows, significantly impeded the political cohesion of the three major ethnic groups in national politics, it may be time for Nigeria to move back toward a more economical and consolidated federal system with fewer units but more real devolution of power. This is, in fact, one of the options being advanced (along with various proposals for a much more radically decentralized confederation) as Nigeria prepares at this writing to begin a Constitutional Conference to discuss its future political structures. Yet true federalism can never be realized under military rule, which is intrinsically centralizing. We strongly agree with Suberu that democracy, despite all of its flaws and imperfections, offers possibilities for consensus-building, constitutional adaptation, and political learning that render it far superior to military rule in its potential to control ethnic conflict.

If Nigeria, with its now endlessly protracted military rule, is a leading negative example, India, with its elaborate federalism and far-reaching constitutional protections for individual and minority rights, continues to stand as a signal positive demonstration of the effectiveness of democratic principles in the management of ethnic conflict. Democracy in India, more perhaps than in any other country in the world, has benefitted from the highly dispersed, decentralized, complex, and densely cross-cutting character of its multiple lines of ethnic, religious, and caste cleavage. This character figured prominently in the reversal of the electoral fortunes of the Hindu fundamentalist Bharatiya Janata Party (BJP) in November 1993, when a successful political coalescence of lower castes, ex-untouchables, and Muslims against "upper-caste communalism" dealt the BJP surprising defeats in three of four states in the "Hindi heartland."[32] But it has not precluded all manner of intense and often violent ethnic movements. In dampening these centrifugal tendencies and limiting their impact on the national polity, however, India's federalism and constitutionalism have played crucial roles. Indeed, India's worst ethnic traumas since partition—the murderous conflicts in Punjab and Kashmir, and the more general rise of violent tribal and ethnoregional movements—were aggravated if not largely generated by usurpations of state autonomy and various abuses of central power that began in earnest under Indira Gandhi. Hardgrave pointedly argues that the balance between the center and the states must be restored if India is to overcome its current turmoil.

One of the most vexing issues in the management of ethnic conflict involves the last of Horowitz's five mechanisms for conflict reduction— reducing disparities between ethnic groups. Here, too, every initiative has its potential costs and dangers. Witness the considerable support for Hindu fundamentalist politics offered by urban upper castes who have been threatened or displaced by India's varied and complex affirmative-action provisions, which now "reserve" 49 percent of all federal government jobs for historically disadvantaged groups.[33] Both our Nigerian and Indian case studies point out how inflexible quotas for disadvantaged groups can actually reinforce group consciousness and generate explosive grievances by those groups that view themselves as victims of "reverse discrimination." Hardgrave suggests that India target individual economic need more than caste status as the basis for special employment and educational opportunities. Suberu urges that Nigeria redirect investment to redress the roots of educational inequality between north and south, rather than preclude fair competition for government jobs through the current system of quotas. Horowitz has expressed a similar and more general skepticism about such preferential policies, particularly when they are rigid. He highlights not only the problem of misplaced targeting (which may only widen disparities between classes *within* ethnic groups), but also considerations of time. Equity gains (if any) tend to be far off in the future, but the chief aim "of these policies is to reduce disparities in the present, and it is in the present that the costs show up" in terms of weakened performance incentives, perverse reinforcements of a group's inability to compete, corruption, intense ethnic backlashes, and hence increased ethnic conflict.[34]

Finally, ethnic-conflict management must be considered in an international context. In Kashmir, Sri Lanka, Bosnia, and throughout Eastern Europe and the former Soviet Union, ethnic conflicts and insurgencies are intertwined with the strong national, religious, and linguistic bonds that unite peoples across borders. Neighboring states, and more broadly the international community, have a critical role to play in ensuring that minorities are treated fairly and that states which do respect individual and group rights can feel secure within their borders. Bugajski urges East European governments "to conclude bilateral agreements with neighbors, mutually guaranteeing the rights of resident minorities and renouncing any territorial pretensions." This strategy holds promise for reducing ethnic conflict around the world, as does Bugajski's suggestion that regional and international organizations like the CSCE and the United Nations actively monitor and formally codify minority rights, as well as mediate interethnic disputes.

Although the essays in this collection raise disturbing political and moral issues, they do not counsel despair. Just as unsuitable institutions and irresponsible leadership can generate horrifying explosions of ethnic violence and terror, so can wise incentives and political restraint and accommodation return societies to some level of peace and civility. If there is an overarching message from all the chapters that follow, it is the value of democracy for controlling the worst impulses of ethnicity and nationalism, but also the importance of structuring democracy properly and in timely fashion for that purpose. Just as the abuse of federalism fed the Punjab crisis in India, so (as Hardgrave observes) the restoration of self-rule there has greatly eased it. For all its continuing ethnic tensions and violence, and for all its increasing distortions, federalism in Nigeria has been the single most important factor preventing the recurrence of civil war. Certainly the continued existence of Canada as a single state would have been unthinkable without its deeply institutionalized commitments to democracy and federalism. Where political institutions that disperse power, protect minorities, and reward moderation are planted early enough, democracy and peace can prevail. As Horowitz observed a decade ago, and as our contributors ably confirm, "Even in the most severely divided society, ties of blood do not ineluctably lead to rivers of blood."[35]

NOTES

1. Hans Kohn, *The Idea of Nationalism: A Study in Its Origin and Background* (New York: Macmillan, 1944); Ernest Gellner, *Nations and Nationalism* (Ithaca, N.Y.: Cornell University Press, 1983); Elie Kedourie, *Nationalism*, 4th ed. (Oxford: Blackwell, 1993); Anthony D. Smith, *Theories of Nationalism*, 2nd ed. (London: Duckworth, 1983).

2. Jean-Jacques Rousseau, *Second Discourse*, in Roger D. Masters, ed., *The First and Second Discourses* (New York: St. Martin's, 1964), 79.

3. Kohn, op. cit., 23; and E.H. Carr et al., *Nationalism: A Report by a Study Group of Members of the Institute of International Affairs* (London: Oxford University Press, 1939), 27.

4. Gellner, op. cit., 1.

5. Jean-Jacques Rousseau, *Considérations sur le gouvernement de Pologne*, in *Ouevres complètes*, 4 vols., published under the direction of Bernard Gagnebin and Marcel Raymond (Paris: Gallimard, Bibliothèque de la Pléiade, 1959-69), 3:960 (translation ours).

6. Ibid., 970-71.

7. For a further discussion of Rousseau's treatment of nationalism, see Marc F. Plattner, "Rousseau and the Origins of Nationalism," in Clifford Orwin and Nathan Tarcov, eds., *The Legacy of Rousseau* (Chicago: University of Chicago Press, forthcoming).

8. Donald Horowitz, *Ethnic Groups in Conflict* (Berkeley: University of California Press, 1985), ch. 6, esp. 267.

9. Harold R. Isaacs, *Idols of the Tribe: Group Identity and Political Change* (New York: Harper & Row, 1975), 3.

10. Horowitz, op. cit., 53.

11. G. Bingham Powell, *Contemporary Democracies: Participation, Stability and Violence* (Cambridge, Mass.: Harvard University Press, 1982), 43.

12. Horowitz, op. cit., 224.

13. Ibid., 219-24.

14. Donald Horowitz, "Ethnic Conflict Management for Policymakers," in Joseph V. Montville, ed., *Conflict and Peacemaking in Multiethnic Societies* (Lexington, Mass.: Lexington Books, 1990), 115-16.

15. Alvin Rabushka and Kenneth Shepsle, *Politics in Plural Societies: A Theory of Democratic Instability* (Columbus, Ohio: Charles E. Merrill), 62-92.

16. Robert A. Dahl, *Polyarchy: Participation and Opposition* (New Haven: Yale University Press, 1971), 108-11; Rupert Emerson, "The Prospects for Democracy," in Michael F. Lofchie, ed., *The State of the Nations* (Berkeley: University of California Press, 1971), 248-49; Michael T. Hannan and Glenn P. Carrol, "Dynamics of Formal Political Structure: An Event-History Analysis," *American Sociological Review* 46 (January 1981): 19-35.

17. Powell, op. cit., 40-53, 157.

18. Dahl, op. cit., 36-40.

19. Ibid., 44.

20. Seymour Martin Lipset, *Political Man: The Social Bases of Politics* (Baltimore: Johns Hopkins University Press, 1979), 70-79.

21. Horowitz, *Ethnic Groups in Conflict*, 7-8.

22. *Human Rights Watch World Report 1994* (New York: Human Rights Watch, December 1993), 13.

23. Susanne Hoeber Rudolph and Lloyd I. Rudolph, "Modern Hate," *The New Republic*, 22 March 1993, 26.

24. Avoiding the indefinite exclusion of any group from the opportunity to participate in the governing coalition at the center is Dahl's first condition for maintaining ethnic conflicts "at a low enough level to sustain a polyarchy" (Dahl, op. cit., 114-18).

25. Arend Lijphart, *Democracy in Plural Societies* (New Haven: Yale University Press, 1977); idem, *Democracies: Patterns of Majoritarian and Consensus Government in Twenty-One Countries* (New Haven: Yale University Press, 1984); and idem, "The Power-Sharing Approach," in Montville, ed., 491-509.

26. Donald Horowitz, "Making Moderation Pay: The Comparative Politics of Ethnic Conflict Management," in Montville, ed., op. cit., 451-476.

27. Larry Diamond, "Political Corruption: Nigeria's Perennial Struggle," *Journal of Democracy* 2 (Fall 1991): 73-85.

28. Larry Diamond, "Nigeria's Search for a New Political Order," *Journal of Democracy* 2 (Spring 1991): 62-63.

29. Horowitz, *Ethnic Groups in Conflict*, 635-38.

30. Ibid., 598.

31. Ibid., 598-99.

32. Lloyd I. Rudolph and Susanne Hoeber Rudolph, "Unholy Rao," *The New Republic*, 14 February 1994, 18.

33. In addition to Hardgrave, see Rudolph and Rudolph, "Modern Hate," 29.

34. Horowitz, *Ethnic Groups in Conflict*, 660-80; quote is from 660.

35. Ibid., 684.

I.
Nationalism and Democracy

1.
NATIONALISM
AND DEMOCRACY

Ghia Nodia

Ghia Nodia is head of the department of political philosophy at the Institute of Philosophy in Tbilisi, Georgia. He wrote this essay at the Kennan Institute for Advanced Russian Studies of the Woodrow Wilson Center in Washington, D.C., where he was a research scholar during the 1991-92 academic year.

The collapse of communism in Eastern Europe and the former Soviet Union has led simultaneously to dramatic new gains for liberal democracy and to a resurgence of nationalism. Many analysts appear to regard these as contradictory phenomena, inasmuch as they consider nationalism to be fundamentally antidemocratic. I believe that this is a superficial view that distorts our understanding of what is happening in the postcommunist countries and elsewhere as well. In any case, the experience of the anticommunist revolution requires us to rethink not only the relationship between nationalism and democracy, but also many of the other basic ideas on which modern civilization is grounded.

The first major attempt at such a rethinking appeared on the very cusp of the great change when Francis Fukuyama's meditation on the "end of history" was published in the summer of 1989.[1] Fukuyama's main idea, later developed at book length, was that the disintegration of communism left the idea of liberal democracy standing alone, with no viable ideological competitor in sight.[2] Thus the posthistorical stage of human development, boring though it may be, has arrived, and there is no threat to the reign of liberal democracy.

Although I generally agree with Fukuyama's analysis, I do not share his mostly negative assessment of the role of nationalism in the advent, spread, and victory of liberal democracy. To put it simply, Fukuyama (despite occasional equivocations) agrees with the predominant Western view that democracy and nationalism are mutually hostile.[3] If one wins, it can do so only at the other's expense. Democracy, moreover, has become a term linked to adjectives like "good," "civilized," "progressive," "rational," and so on, while nationalism is associated with "backwardness," "immaturity," "barbarism," "irrationality," and the like. Given these valuations, Fukuyama's presumption that "irrationalist" nationalism does not present a viable alternative to democracy, and that history has thus come to a safe end, marks him as an optimist. Meanwhile, pessimists like Shlomo Avineri argue that nationalism, not liberal democracy, is the real successor to communism, which means that history will continue.[4]

But what if nationalism and democracy are not two separate things? What if nationalism is a *component* of the more complex entity that is called "liberal democracy"? In raising these questions, I mean to suggest that the idea of nationalism is impossible—indeed unthinkable—without the idea of democracy, and that democracy never exists without nationalism. The two are joined in a sort of complicated marriage, unable to live without each other, but coexisting in an almost permanent state of tension. Divorce might seem the logical solution to a Western liberal horrified by the twentieth century's experience of European nationalism, but this option stands revealed as nothing more than wishful thinking once real political forces are taken into account.

The manner in which the collapse of communism and the breakup of the Soviet empire occurred tends to demonstrate the validity of my approach. Conversely, the failure of mainstream Western political science to keep pace with developments in the postcommunist East is at least partly due to the West's one-sided understanding of nationalism and its relation to democracy.

This one-sidedness flows largely from Western social science's tendencies toward both economic determinism and value-laden judgments. When it is presumed that social developments cannot be explained in a really "scientific" way unless they can be traced to economic conditions, it is only a small step to the modern instrumentalist doctrine according to which nations and nationalisms emerge as a result of 1) industrialization and 2) mass manipulation undertaken by elites pursuing their own (ultimately economic) interests. This "scientistic" attitude, however, does not prevent many of the very same scholars who assume it from using "democracy" and "nationalism" as valuative rather than descriptive terms. Democracy is cast in the hero's role, and is not supposed to have anything in common with the nationalist villain.

Of course, no social scientist can completely avoid value preferences. I myself, for instance, agree with Winston Churchill that democracy is a very bad political system with one very good justification: all the others are worse. Still, the valuative attitude is incompatible with the theoretical one. As a theorist, I cannot be interested in whether nationalism is "good" or "bad"; what is important is that it exists. On the other hand—and here I agree with Fukuyama—social reality does not depend solely on objective data; subjective human attitudes that defy all attempts at reductionism can and do exist. This is a truth that we ought to keep in mind as we try to understand the relationship between democracy and nationalism.

It is essential to begin our analysis of nationalism and democracy by making certain distinctions. First, while "democracy" is often used interchangeably with "liberal democracy," the latter combines two distinct ideas, liberalism and democracy, whose compatibility is not as obvious as it may seem today to the average Western citizen. There is some difference and even tension between the two, which leads them to have differing attitudes toward nationalism.

Second, we must be sure not to overlook the important difference between *emerging* democracies (which often are found in newly emerging states) and established democratic regimes existing in states with long traditions of uninterrupted sovereignty. Nationalism works differently in each of these two types of countries. Taking these two distinctions together, one could say that the test of *mature* democracy consists in achieving the right mixture of liberal and democratic principles, while the birth pangs characteristic of emerging democracy betoken an effort to arrive at such a compromise.

The third distinction that I think is meaningful here is between "homegrown" and "imported" liberal democracies. Modern democracy first emerged in northwestern Europe and North America. Later the democratic model began to spread throughout the world and now, after having defeated communism in the Cold War, it seems to have won near-universal recognition. But are the historical preconditions and mechanisms that explain the original emergence of democracy the same as those that account for its dissemination? Is the relation between liberal and democratic principles the same in "indigenous" and "imported" democracies? Is nationalism's role the same in both cases? The answer to this last question, I think, is no. Keeping this in mind will also be helpful.

Finally, we must remember that we are now witnessing something that has absolutely no precedent in history: the transition to liberal democracy after communism. All previous transitions were from more traditional societies. Does this make any essential difference for the role of nationalism in democratic transitions? I think that it does.

The Logic of Democracy

At the core of democracy is the principle of popular sovereignty, which holds that government can be legitimated only by the will of those whom it governs. This general principle has to be distinguished from democratic *procedures*, which are intended as devices for discerning what the people really will. The main procedure is, of course, elections. Other sets of procedures help to safeguard democracy by restraining elected rulers through such measures as the separation of powers, limits on reelection, special requirements for constitutional amendments, and so on.

Democracy is supposed to be a highly *rational* enterprise. Its debt to the rationalist philosophical tradition can be easily seen in the notion of the social contract, which conceives of society as the construct of free and calculating individuals bent on maximizing their own interests. Democracy is a system of rules legitimated by the will of the people; it is presumed that the people will generally choose what seems to be in their best interest.

Thus anything that seems insufficiently rational, be it irrationalist philosophy or irrational human sentiments, is commonly understood as contrary to the idea of democracy. Nationalism is only one example of an "irrational" phenomenon that supposedly cuts against the democratic grain. By arguing that there is a necessary and positive link between nationalism and democracy, I am of course flying in the face of this common understanding.

To see how a nonrational phenomenon like nationalism can be vital to the democratic enterprise, it is helpful to compare this enterprise to a game. Democracy, like any game, consists of rules whose validity depends solely on the willingness of a certain community (the players, or citizens) to observe them. This analogy corresponds well to both of the aspects of democracy that we mentioned: the principle of popular sovereignty, and the fact that this sovereignty can meaningfully express itself only insofar as a specific set of rules (the constitution and laws) is created in its name. Popular sovereignty consists in the claim that "We the People" are going to play only by rules that we ourselves freely choose. Such rules (unlike the rules of games) are usually thought to have some independent moral value, which may in turn be grounded on certain religious beliefs ("In God We Trust"). But the concrete manner of *interpreting* those universal values (or God's will) depends on individual believers—on "We the People." Thus does democracy differ in principle from political systems (whether traditional or modern) where some ruling elite interprets the divine will (or an equivalent, like Marx's "laws" of historical development) and hands down rules accordingly.

This "game-like" aspect of democracy supposedly shows it to be completely rational. If we push the analogy further, however, we uncover nonrational aspects of the democratic enterprise. In addition to rules, a game also requires a community of players and a playing field. In games, all these things are wholly conventional and arbitrary, but this is not the case with the democratic enterprise. Democratic laws ("the rules") may be consensual products of rational decision making, but the composition and territory of the polity (the "players" and the "playing field") in which these laws will have force cannot be defined that way. Democracy, of course, has standard categories (citizenship and borders) for defining the players and the playing field. But the criteria for deciding just who is a citizen and just where the borders are cannot be derived from any logic intrinsic to the democratic enterprise.

Successful democracy presupposes the settling of these questions, whether or not the logic of rational democratic action has any inner resources for solving them. It is true that the democratic principle of self-determination and the democratic procedure of voting may help to facilitate their resolution, but the logic of democracy itself provides no specific criteria to guide one's vote or identify just which people and territories are to be included in the polity. Why should or should not a given group of people in a given area join or secede from some larger political entity?

Since the idea of democracy is universal, it would only be logical for the principle of popular sovereignty to be embodied in a worldwide polity. But this assumes that the democratic transition should be worldwide in the first place, and that the people themselves want it that way. History bears out neither of these assumptions. Democracy has always emerged in distinct communities; there is no record anywhere of free, unconnected, and calculating individuals coming together spontaneously to form a democratic social contract *ex nihilo*. Whether we like it or not, nationalism is the historical force that has provided the political units for democratic government. "Nation" is another name for "We the People."

Constructing Nations

Traditional European nationalism tried to formulate objective marks of nationhood that would enable any given unit of people to provide a rational justification of its demand for "self-determination." These could include language, common origin, historical tradition of statehood, or the like, and could—or so it was hoped—place the democratic edifice on a completely rational foundation. There would exist universally valid objective criteria defining a "fair" distribution of territory among peoples; groups or individuals with doubts about their membership in a given nation could find just and impartial standards for resolving them. But the actual history of nationalisms, to say nothing of the theoretical critiques offered by scholars like Hans Kohn and Ernest Gellner, has shown that such objective and universal criteria are unattainable.[5] The development of premodern ethnic communities into modern nations has always been mediated by historical contingencies and conscious political effort; there simply are no God-given or naturally preordained national borders.

However much this discovery may have undermined nationalism's claim to provide universally valid rational criteria, it did not change nationalism's function of molding democratic (i.e., self-determining) political communities. The criteria by which nations are distinguished from one another may not pass the test of universal objective validity, but the political cohesion necessary for democracy cannot be achieved without the people determining themselves to be "the nation."

The less than fully rational character of the nationalist principle can shake the foundations of democracy and even give rise to bloodshed. In the absence of universally valid criteria of nationhood, conflicts arise which are not always susceptible to fair and rational solutions. It is hard to find even an island nation that has not had some sort of territorial dispute with its neighbors. The typical means of resolving such conflicts is war. Many nations must deal with ethnic minorities who are distrusted as potential traitors and who in turn view the majority as would-be oppressors. There are different means of resolving these problems: radical "final" solutions like genocide or expulsion; gradualist solutions like assimilation; or compromise solutions, like various schemes for communal or regional autonomy within a federal state. Only rarely can solutions be reached without pain and violence, which is why so many supporters of modern democracy devoutly wish to avoid the nationalist principle. Wishes, however, cannot dictate reality.

Attempts to deny the reality and significance of nationalism often stem from a reluctance to admit that the democratic enterprise, supposedly the epitome of rationality, rests unavoidably on a nonrational foundation. The early stages of democracy-building make it especially clear that a nonrational act of political definition (determining who belongs to "We the People") is a necessary precondition of rational political behavior. The failure to recognize this kept most Western intellectuals from understanding what was really happening in (or rather to) the Soviet Union during *perestroika*. Their warnings about nationalism as a major obstacle to democratic reform ignored the truth that all *real* democratic movements (save the one in Russia proper) were at the same time nationalist. Leaders from independence-minded republics were asked what they hoped to gain economically from independence, while the would-be nations themselves saw sovereignty as an end in itself rather than as a mere means to prosperity.

The interdependence between democracy and nationalism expresses itself in still another way. Modern democratic regimes, no less than modern nations, are artificial constructs. Premodern democracy was tied exclusively to the *polis*, the classical city-state. This democracy was essentially commensurate with human personality: the site of the democratic enterprise was small, and citizens dealt with one another face-to-face. Modern democracy extends far beyond such intimate boundaries, and so requires citizens to develop a sense of community that is based less on their unaided senses and more on the human mind or imagination.[6] For the most part, modern nations and modern democracies alike are too large to do without this "imagined" quality.

Eugen Weber's noted study *Peasants into Frenchmen* shows how, at the time of the French Revolution (from which the French nation in the

modern sense stems), few rural folk in the largely rural society of the
ancien *régime* thought of themselves as being distinctly
"French"—indeed, many of them did not even speak French.[7] Cohesion
was the fruit of a deliberate, centralized, and at times harsh political
effort; the French nation that resulted is more "artificial" than "natural."
The book's title could as well be *Peasants into Citizens*, which would
highlight the paradox involved in making citizens ("city-dwellers") out
of peasants (*paysans* or "country people") without taking them to the
city. Such is the paradox upon which the possibility of modern
democracy is based, for democracy, which is an urban phenomenon to
begin with, had to spread throughout the country (meaning the
countryside, where most people still lived at the dawn of
democratization). This could only be accomplished through a conscious
political effort, whether undertaken by centralized state bureaucracies,
cultural elites, or others. In fact, the transformation of peasants into
Frenchmen and citizens was a single process. Peasants could be made
into Frenchmen only by becoming citizens, and vice versa: the two
moments are divisible in theory, but not in practice.[8]

Thus the demands of democracy-building provide incentives for
molding nations out of preexistent ethnic material. Saying, as Ernest
Gellner does, that "nationalism engenders nations" also implies that
democratic transitions (and not just industrialism or capitalism) engender
nations.[9] That is why, in emergent democracies, movements for
democracy and movements for independence are often one and the same.
Both are acting in the name of "self-determination": "We the People"
(i.e., the nation) will decide our own fate; we will observe only those
rules that we ourselves set up; and we will allow nobody—whether
absolute monarch, usurper, or foreign power—to rule us without our
consent.

This argument applies with special force in the case of emerging
democracies, where nationalism is needed to get the democratic enterprise
started. The role of national feeling in *sustaining* this enterprise is
different. Once democracies feel stable and secure within their own
borders, national feeling may gradually begin to decline in intensity and
significance. One may argue whether or not something like this is
happening in Western Europe today, but that is a different issue.

Liberalism versus Nationalism

Most denunciations of nationalism in the name of democracy are
actually denunciations of nationalism in the name of *liberalism*. By
liberalism, I mean that doctrine which holds individual human liberty to
be the foremost political value. Nationalism, on the other hand, gives
preference to collective claims based on race, culture, or some other
communal identity. Liberalism champions a person's right to *choose*,

while nationalism gives pride of place to something that does not depend on personal choice.

The controversy, however, is about more than value preferences. The basic liberal critique of nationalism is that the nation is "unreal" ("imagined," "created," "concocted," etc.), while the individual human person is completely "real." Closely tied to this view is the notion that the individual (the bearer of inalienable rights) is "rational," while the nation is "irrational." Nations are held to be irrational and unreal because, as we saw earlier, there exist no universally objective criteria of nationhood. Fukuyama presents one justification for this differentiation:

> The distinction between human and nonhuman is fully rational: only human beings are free, that is, able to struggle for recognition in a battle for pure prestige. This distinction is based on nature, or rather, on the radical disjunction between the realm of nature and the realm of freedom. The distinction between one human group and another, on the other hand, is an accidental and arbitrary by-product of human history.[10]

This passage shows how shaky is liberalism's claim to be *rationally* grounded. The distinction between human and nonhuman is "rational" in the sense that it is evident and may be described in "natural" terms. But the tricky thing is that the claim for universal recognition of man as man (which Fukuyama and I agree is the core of liberalism) is not based merely on the disjunction between the human and nonhuman realms. What the doctrine of personal "dignity" rests on is not just the *fact* that man is different, but the idea that there is something in this difference which is of absolute *value*. Yet this value is not empirically evident or "natural." Fukuyama himself admits, following Hegel, that the claim for universal personal recognition is based upon Christianity, which he calls a "slave ideology" (unlike a "master ideology," which would imply recognition for masters only).[11] It was Christianity that ascribed a sort of transcendent value exclusively to the human soul. If Christianity, however, is merely an "ideology" (which means that it is by definition false), then the case for universal human recognition rests on a false premise, and thus it certainly cannot be called "natural" or "rational." Of course, it is not necessary to be a Christian believer in order to be a human person with human dignity, but neither is it indispensable to claim that my demand for recognition of the value of my personal freedom is based on some "rational" (in the sense of scientifically provable) considerations.

Although liberal democracy may owe many of its victories to the progress of scientific rationality, neither democratic nor liberal *principles* are based on a rational foundation. Both may be described as "nonrational" or "prerational" (but not necessarily "irrational," which usually means hostile to rationality). Value preferences in this case (as,

I think, in all other cases) must ultimately be based only on faith (much as Christian belief is) rather than on rational knowledge.

It is true that the modern instrumentalist teaching on the contingent character of nations has exploded the nationalist myth of the nation as a nonhistorical entity directly rooted in some transcendent or natural order. Yet none of this makes the nation "unreal" for an ordinary man born into a concrete society, culture, and state, and faced with concrete choices on the social and political as well as the spiritual and existential planes. The nation need not be "rational" in order to be "real."

Nationhood and Personality

So far, we have said nothing to contradict the conventional wisdom that liberalism and nationalism are mutually exclusive principles between which one must choose. Let us ask, then, whether there is not some *positive* link between liberalism and nationalism, as well as between the idea of nationhood and that of human personality. That both ideas are tied to the historical epoch of modernity is no accident. Their relation is not only mediated by "objective" mechanisms of modernization; the real connection between them should be traced back to the modern paradigm of thought, from which liberal ideology stems.

At the center of the modern paradigm is the concept of the autonomous human personality. The bearer of a unique and transcendent value (in Kant's terms, it is always the end and should never become a means), this personality is only willing to follow rules endorsed by its own decision (self-determination). Although this idea is often said to have necessarily atheistic implications, it flows historically from the Christian tradition. In principle, moreover, it is possible for an autonomous human being to affirm the existence of an absolute divine order even while maintaining that the interpretation of that order and the application of its precepts to specific cases belong finally to the reason and moral conscience of the individual rather than to any community or institution.[12]

The concept of nationhood also has an intrinsic link to this idea of personality, which is what distinguishes modern self-conscious nationalism from primordial ethnicity. The essence of ethnicity lies in its extension of the idea of *family* to the macrosocial level. Community is "imagined" as a big family stemming from the same ancestor. When a nation "imagines" itself, however, it sees not a family, but a unique personality with a distinct character.

National self-consciousness is patterned on the blueprint of individual human personality in two ways. First, a nation is a community of people organized around the idea of *self-determination*. A modern nation, like a modern self-conscious individual (and unlike an ancient *ethnos*), observes only those laws which it endorses for itself and rejects rules imposed by an external force. Secondly, a nation no less than an individual person requires partners for interaction and mutual recognition. Nations need other nations. A nation can understand and recognize itself only in the context of the history of humanity as such—an idea that is completely unthinkable for even the most advanced ethnic consciousness (for example, that of the ancient Greeks). The idea of nationhood is an idea of membership in humanity, and the idea of humanity as a "family of nations" has long been a mainstay of liberal nationalism.

The conceptual linkage between nationhood and personality has an important corollary. A nation demands self-determination not as an exclusive privilege, but as a way of realizing the general proposition that each nation deserves a state of its own. I do not understand why Fukuyama thinks that nationalism is by definition "megalothymic" (demanding of greater recognition), while holding that liberal individualism is by definition "isothymic" (demanding of equal recognition). Nationalism in its proper sense does not, as Fukuyama claims, "extend recognition only to members of a given national or ethnic group."[13] This attitude is better covered by such terms as "racism" or "chauvinism." Nor does nationalism demand recognition only for *individual* members of a given national or ethnic group. What it demands is recognition for the nation *as a whole*, which means acquiring the general hallmark of nationhood: legal status as an independent state (comparable to the legal status of citizenship in the case of an individual) and acceptance as an equal member of the "family of nations." The basic idea of nationalism is at least as isothymic as that of individualist personalism, even though nations, like individuals, can become megalothymic.

Another sign of the kinship between liberalism and nationalism is that both are often criticized for the same thing: being divisive. The atomized individualism associated with liberalism divides the community, it is said, while nationalism divides humanity. Both accusations are accurate in a sense, but both overlook the record of practical achievement which shows liberalism and nationalism to be the most effective *unifying* forces known to history.

Liberal individualism is emotionally divisive, but only liberal societies have achieved stable civil peace, while "warm" communal ideologies often end up fomenting bloodshed. Attempts to unite the world in the name of universalist doctrines like Christianity (I mean Christianity as a *political* force) and communism have only led to international hostilities. Although plenty of blood has been shed for the sake of "national interests," the first organization to embrace almost the whole world is called the United Nations (not the Universal Church or the Communist International), and it is based on isothymic nationalism ("respect for national sovereignty," "inviolability of borders," etc.). The general principles of nationalism still seem more widely accepted around the globe than those of liberalism or any other ideology.[14] The part of the world that invented nationalism—Western Europe—has also outrun all other regions in defining new patterns of international unity. Europe has reached this unprecedented degree of comity not by neglecting nationalism, as many believe, but by cultivating its isothymic aspect. Independent states voluntarily give up more and more of their sovereignty *because* it is respected. The movement from megalothymia to isothymia is possible not only on the individual but also on the national level.

The Liberal Dilemma

Although most liberals since World War II have denounced nationalism as a barbarous atavism, the classical liberals of the nineteenth century harbored more complicated attitudes. On the theoretical level, nothing in the liberal principle requires an acceptance of the principle of nationhood at all, for to a true liberal the autonomous human person is *the* decisive unit of analysis. The liberal attitude toward nationalism, however, is mediated by the liberal attitude toward the *state*.

All states unavoidably involve some sort of domination or repression—things that liberals naturally dislike. They regard the state as a necessary evil, acceptable only because its absence is even worse for the individual. Thus do liberals make their peace with the state—the only force capable of preventing the war of all against all and guaranteeing individual rights.

The key question, then, is what kind of state? Today it seems self-evident that liberals should prefer the democratic state above all others. But liberals did not come to that conclusion right away. Why not, for instance, back a decent enlightened monarchy? After all, the social base of liberalism has always been elitist-aristocratic (if not in the hereditary at least in the moral-intellectual sense). Liberals have always feared the *demos* as a threat to freedom.[15] The tyranny of the majority—and hence of mediocrity—is an inherent danger of democracy. But in the end liberals came to loathe the tyranny of blood over soul and the arbitrariness of dynastic rulers even more, and so embraced democracy; in doing so, they had to respect, even to some extent follow, the general will. Yet as we have seen, this will could not help being more or less nationalistic.

The dilemma that this presented is vividly expressed in the works of great nineteenth-century liberals like John Stuart Mill and Lord Acton. Mill was not an emotional nationalist; rather he was a firm advocate of *democratic* liberalism who reasoned that "free institutions are next to impossible in a country made up of different nationalities. . . . [I]t is in general a necessary condition for free institutions that the boundaries of governments should coincide in the main with those of nationalities."[16]

Having endorsed democracy, Mill found that he had no choice but to endorse nationalism.

Lord Acton, on the other hand, was an outspoken opponent of the nationality principle, which he regarded as incompatible with personal liberty. In contrast to Mill, he thought that "the combination of different nations in one state is as necessary a condition of civilized life as the combination of men and women in society."[17] This logically led him to a qualified acceptance of racism and imperial rule.[18] He also came close to rejecting democracy, denouncing the Rousseauan principle of equality as a doctrine no less false than those of communism or nationalism.[19] Much to the discomfiture of aristocratic liberals like Lord Acton, peoples themselves, when it is up to them, always begin building democracy by creating independent nation-states that may wind up being less friendly to personal freedom than the *ancien régime* was.

Nowadays the People, having turned into the middle class, no longer seem very dangerous. Still, liberals reject nationalism more strongly than ever. Why?

There are, of course, various reasons for this. The role played by nationalist extremism in our century's two horrific world wars has had a powerful impact. The decolonization of the post-World War II period made "national self-determination" a predominantly Third World problem, thus reinforcing the liberal tendency to associate nationalism with "backwardness."

The old liberal fear of the people is still there, I think, although with the option of enlightened absolutism no longer available, a liberal cannot afford to be openly antidemocratic. Fear of the people, therefore, takes the more respectable form of aversion to nationalism. When a kind of benign *ancien régime* seemed about to emerge from the decay of Soviet communism, Western liberals preferred that regime's unelected enlightened monarch, Mikhail Gorbachev, to the popularly elected but rough-hewn Boris Yeltsin (a leader who seemed as unpredictable as the people who put him in power), not to mention the democratically legitimate nationalist leaders in other republics.

The Two Sides of Nationalism

Despite all that we have said about nationalism's theoretical affinities with both democracy and liberalism, it is undeniable that nationalism in practice has often been illiberal and sometimes antidemocratic.

Nationalism is a coin with two sides: one is political, the other ethnic. There have been attempts to present these as two different kinds of nationalism, one "good" and the other "bad."[20] But these are only ideal types; in reality, nationalism is always *both* political *and* ethnic, although one aspect may predominate to varying degrees. The idea of nationhood is political, and there is no nationalism without a political element. But its substance is irreducibly ethnic. The relationship may be expressed as one of a political soul animating an ethnic body.

The illiberal flesh of ethnicity cannot be wholly denied, but it can be tamed if dealt with reasonably. Ethnic pride in common ancestors, a glorious history, great traditions, a shared language, a noble culture, and so on, can be sublimated into patriotic esteem for the institutions and achievements created by a democratic (not just ethnic) "we." The United States presents a pattern of this sublimation: national pride focuses on the "American way of life," the country's free and stable institutions, and its role as the "leader of the free world." Patriotic celebration of such things may grate on the sensibilities of individualistic liberals, but it offers no threat to ethnic minorities. On the contrary, a custom of tolerance for minorities can also become a point of national pride, as it has in the case of many Americans or citizens of other long-established democratic nations.

Failure to tame the ethnic flesh of nationalism can lead to chauvinism, racism, or even fascism. Yet these manifestations of nationalism's ugly side arise not from excessive ethnicity but from the lack of a robust political expression for national feeling. When they have no political or institutional achievements to take pride in, people may boast instead of their inherited racial, linguistic, or cultural identities.

These reflections point us toward consideration of the different role played by nationalism in "homegrown" and "imported" democracies. The democratic enterprise, as we have seen, requires some principle to mold and inform the body politic; nationalism provides this principle. In the "original" democracies of Western Europe and North America, however, the institutions of free and popular government grew out of gradual, centuries-long developments in culture, society, thought, and economics. Liberal ideas and their socioeconomic and cultural correlates came before political democracy, which was viewed more as a means of restricting power than as an end in itself. Common ethnicity played a quiet role by reinforcing the basic moral and cultural consensus on which the new democratic order was to rest.

Must all nations follow a like path in order to attain stable democracy? Does there exist some common scheme of democratic transition that is followed independently by different countries? Francis Fukuyama thinks that such a scheme does exist, and sketches it as follows: Industrial progress, based on scientific rationality and capitalist economics, "gets us to the gates of the Promised Land of liberal democracy, but it does not quite deliver us to the other side." What makes humankind take that final step is "a totally noneconomic drive, the *struggle for recognition*"—or, in other words, the sense of human dignity.[21] Economic prosperity may be achieved without proper provision being made for the equal recognition of human dignity; prosperous people will eventually begin to chafe at this, however, and will use their resources (wealth, education, etc.) to press for democratic reform. Thus certain socioeconomic preconditions (including "a strong sense of national unity") make a country ripe for democracy, while the desire for equal personal recognition carries it to fruition.[22]

In general, Fukuyama's scheme is accurate. Industrial development and free enterprise are necessary for stable and balanced democracy. But it is far from certain that all countries have to wait until they are "ripe" for democracy before taking the final step. Rare are the cases like those in East Asia or Chile where the socioeconomic conditions needed for democracy were met before authoritarian regimes were dismantled like so much useless scaffolding. Rather, democracy has more often been spread in a much less rational way—like a contagion or the latest fashion from Paris. Having established itself in a certain part of the world, it by and by became attractive to other peoples (why it became so alluring is a different issue).

Nationalism has played a crucial twofold role in the diffusion of democracy, a role corresponding to its twofold nature as both political and ethnic. What Fukuyama calls "thymotic pride," and in particular its isothymic aspect, surely provides the final push toward liberal democracy, but it is rooted in national as well as individual dignity. The creation of a liberal democratic polity becomes a measure of political maturity. Failure would signal a shameful "national disgrace." Only sovereign states with stable, liberal democratic governments are eligible to join the prestigious international club of "advanced" or "modern" nations. Otherwise, a country may (at best) be *feared*, as the former Soviet Union was, but it will not be treated with genuine respect.

Still, this kind of sensitivity to "national disgrace" is not experienced in the same way throughout society. It is typically cosmopolitan elites that have absorbed liberal ideas about what a "normal," "civilized" order should look like. With the development of the international media, however, even the broader masses can become sensitive to being "politically backward." It was, after all, a sense of national—and not merely individual—dignity that sent many Russians to the barricades to resist the attempted putsch of August 1991.

In places where democracy came as an "import," the lack of favorable social, economic, spiritual, or cultural conditions created an especially deep chasm between the liberal elites and the great mass of people. The liberal elites were too small and weak to lead the transition movement, and there was no strong middle class to serve as an ally. Moreover, according to the blueprint itself, the transition to modernity had to be made on behalf of the people, who would therefore have to be enticed into political activity. But the foreign doctrine of classical liberalism could not readily be used to mobilize the masses. Accelerated politicization would require more accessible ideologies with far more immediate appeal.

Two offspring of Western liberalism vied to fill this bill: socialism and nationalism. Each competed to sell its own version of modernity to the same customers. There were also numerous attempts to forge a single syncretistic cult out of these two religions of the people, one of which addressed the deity as "class" while the other called it "nation."

Generally speaking, one can say that in "backward" countries the populist and anti-individualist thrust of both socialism and ethnic nationalism tended to loom very large in the absence of those countervailing influences found in the political culture of the West, with its strong civil societies, mass literacy, traditions of tolerance, and stable legal systems. In the absence of these things, the socialist ideal of fairness easily gave way to sheer envy, while nationalism degenerated into a doctrine of "blood and soil."

Given the intrinsic difficulties of nationalist politics that I have already mentioned, these deficiencies and the persistent political failure they portend can stir up waves of frustration powerful enough to sweep the national idea away from its democratic and isothymic moorings and carry it to the far shores of racism and fascism. Nonetheless, denouncing all nationalism as would-be fascism makes no more sense than denouncing all religion for ultimately leading to fanaticism. The problems connected with nationalism are not unique defects stemming from some hapless intellectual error or deliberate fraud, but inherent components of the general problem of democratic transition. Both extreme nationalism and coercive socialism, after all, have usually been tools of accelerated (even if perverse) modernization.

Nationalism after Communism

In the past, the passage to democracy meant the passage away from (though not a total break with) traditional society. In the course of it, some things were rejected, while others were preserved and in a sense provided a basis for modernity.[23] The sense of historical continuity was thus maintained, and the whole development was regarded as a *forward* movement to what is now alleged to be the "end of history." Many of the current democratic transitions, however, are transitions away from communism, and communism is nothing like traditional society. Although it once itself claimed to be the end of history, communism now stands exposed as a historical blind alley.[24] The collapse of communism implies not a movement forward to history's end, but rather a movement *back* to history after a long detour. Returning from this detour, the people of postcommunist lands often believe that communism has created *nothing* useful for or worthy of "civilized" life. So pervasive was communism's penetration of all spheres of life that the prevailing attitude now is one of starting from scratch or building something from nothing.

This renders Fukuyama's scenario of democratization quite irrelevant to postcommunist reality. Of course, the notion that nothing created under communism can be carried into the liberal democratic era is not to be taken literally. Communism did accomplish some tasks of modernization: society was urbanized and educated, railroads and highways were built, etc. All this should not and cannot be reversed or destroyed. Indeed, the growth of literacy and urbanization under communism has improved the odds of successful democratic transition. Among the socioeconomic preconditions of the free society, however, the crucial thing is not just education or urbanization but *private property*. An economic system based on private property is indispensable in helping the individual to establish a healthy balance between freedom and responsibility—a balance on which democracy depends, and which can never be inculcated through theoretical education alone. Urbanized and educated elites may be the driving force of democratic transitions, but they need something to work with.

Postcommunist nations are trying to resume their history from the point where it was interrupted by communism; hence the rejection of communism throughout Eastern Europe and the former Soviet Union necessarily takes the form of attempts at various kinds of restoration and self-recollection. On the other hand, these nations are no longer sealed off behind the Iron Curtain; the rejection of communism also necessarily takes the form of attempts to rejoin the world, a world that has changed greatly since 1918 or 1945. Not surprisingly, the drive to recover one's own identity and the drive to rejoin the outside world have come into conflict; the "true self" to be recovered exists in the past, while the "world" to be joined exists now. This is causing severe collective identity crises and aberrations in the postcommunist nations, and no small amount of bewilderment and confusion in the world at large. The former are making tremendous efforts to rejoin history, only to discover that history has already "ended."

Totalitarianism's decades-long assault on the structures of civil society has left behind a rubble of atomized individuals who are searching frantically for a common principle on which to base their new lives together. In this situation, nationalism comes to the fore as the major—if not the only—principle capable of holding society together. But since the nationalist *political* tradition has been interrupted, the *ethnic* element has become especially strong. This is not to say that no other social forces and ideologies exist: there is religion, there are the pro-Western liberal elites. But everything is somewhat blended with nationalism, or defines itself in relation to it. What is called the "cultural revival" is definitely more national than cultural in the proper sense. The religious revival is more of a national-religious revival: it has so far been more about "unifying the nation" and helping it overcome the alien legacy of atheistic communism than about bringing salvation to individual souls. Appeals to liberal democratic values have power only insofar as these

values can be conflated with *"our* political traditions" or *"our* identity"
as a "Western," "European," or "Christian" culture. On their own, liberal
ideas have almost no prospect of seriously influencing political discourse.

Nationalism is thus both destructive (for communism) and constructive
(by providing unity in a world of disarray); both a grave threat to liberal
democracy, and one of its major sources of hope. Being a "nationalist"
in the postcommunist East can mean almost anything from being a
liberal to being a fascist. Those who say that they reject "nationalism,"
moreover, may only mean to signal their disapproval of ethnic
chauvinism. Many such "antinationalists" are vigorous advocates of
sovereignty for their respective countries. A British activist from the
Liberal International once complained to me that the liberal parties of
Eastern Europe seemed too "right-wing" and nationalistic. Still, I do not
think that Eastern European liberals are necessarily less liberal than their
Western counterparts. What is different is the unavoidably crucial place
of nationalism in postcommunist political discourse, however old-
fashioned it may seem to the contemporary Western mind.

Russians and Others

There is something else that needs to be mentioned here: the
difference between Russians and other former members of the "socialist
camp." Russia was the first to install the communist system; the spread
of communism to other republics of the former Soviet Union, and later
to Eastern and Central Europe, came as a result of Soviet Russian
conquest. In these non-Russian regions, communism was regarded as not
only a politically, but also a *nationally* hostile force—an alien system
imposed by foreign occupiers. Accordingly, overcoming it meant
overcoming the occupation. In part of course, this is fanciful:
communism may have come on Soviet Russian bayonets, but it
penetrated all levels of society deeply enough to make the uprooting of
its legacy a task for generations rather than for a single revolutionary
episode, whether velvet or bloody. Still, there is no denying that
nationalism was a driving force in the movement to topple communism.
Yet seeing the source of evil as an external force can obscure deeper
problems left by communism in one's own society. It also encourages
efforts to place all the blame for totalitarianism on a particular stratum
of society, who are defined as "traitors"; the result may be witch-hunts,
hysterical conspiracy theories, and the like.

As for Russia, the national aspect of postcommunism is even more
complicated there. The tradition of Russian statehood has been the
tradition of an empire; in the Soviet period, this tradition merged with
Russia's role as the leader of the communist world. The spread of
communism and the expansion or reassertion of Russian rule were almost
synonymous (only later did some communist states begin to defect from

Russian domination). It was thanks to communism that Russia reached the peak of its might and influence. The Russian imperial-nationalist tradition converged with the communist principle, leaving Russia with an especially painful postcommunist identity crisis. Russian ethnocultural nationalism was openly anti-Western and therefore antiliberal; although extreme nationalists view communism as a Jewish virus aimed at destroying the Russian people, they have not let that stop them from forming tactical alliances with hard-line Stalinists. As for the Westernizing democrats, they so far have failed to produce any viable and consistent concept of Russian statehood. Their political discourse vacillates between self-denigrating rhetoric about a hapless country of slaves and boasts of renewed national pride that quickly take on imperialistic and authoritarian overtones. A small group regards even the existing Russian Federation as an empire, and is willing to countenance secession by the autonomous republics. The government tends more and more to a pragmatic vision of a "united and inseparable" Russia comprising all the territory contained within the borders of the Russian Federation, but from time to time cannot help making territorial claims on Ukraine and other republics. A nonimperial concept of Russian statehood has yet to be created.

The postcommunist preoccupation with national issues presents real dangers. The problem, however, is not nationalism as some isolated force, a mad demon that must be chained, but rather the general weakness of democracy in postcommunist lands. The demands of transition create a real need for strong executive power, which in turn rouses fears of authoritarianism (few postcommunist leaders avoid accusations of having a dictatorial style). The lack of a strong hand at the helm, however, can lead to anarchy and disarray, which in turn may trigger a bloody and repressive backlash. Since the best available "working" ideology is nationalism, it is only natural that authoritarian tendencies should take on a nationalist cast. Almost all postcommunist countries with sizeable ethnic minorities—which is to say, most postcommunist countries—must face painful problems that pit unstable and insecure majorities against even less secure minorities. Almost all such countries have governments that are guilty, at least by Western standards, of adopting less than perfectly liberal minority policies. I do not see any hope for speedy solutions to the numerous ethnic issues that trouble these countries.

All this rouses quite legitimate fears that the postcommunist world is destined to plunge into a series of wars that will approximately repeat the history of Europe between 1914 and 1945 (which is the period where all the postcommunist countries now exist psychologically). The chief counterbalance is the *presence* of the Western world as a beacon from another and more stable historical era. I stress the word "presence" because I do not have much hope of direct international involvement (mediation efforts, economic sanctions, etc.) in the travails of the postcommunist world. At any rate, such measures have proven to have very limited effects, although in some cases even that is enough to make them wholly justified. The best available counterbalance to the nationalism that lives in the past and fixates on old grievances and old ambitions is an alternative version of the nationalist sentiment that makes it a point of national honor to join the civilized world as an equal and dignified member. A sense of isolation from the comity of nations can be much more painful than any concrete sanction. The civilized world provides adequate (even if imperfect) models not only of flourishing market economies, but of regimes that have struck a real and working balance among the forces of democracy, liberalism, and nationalism. The power of these examples to help the fledgling democracies of the postcommunist world should not be underestimated.

NOTES

1. Francis Fukuyama, "The End of History?" *The National Interest* 16 (Summer 1989), 3-18.

2. Idem, *The End of History and the Last Man* (New York: Free Press, 1992).

3. Ibid., xix, 201-2. For examples of Fukuyama's wavering attitude toward nationalism, cf. 37, 215, and 272. He offers, in effect, three disparate propositions: 1) nationalism contradicts liberal democracy; 2) nationalism does not contradict democracy, and 3) democracy needs nationalism.

4. Shlomo Avineri, "The Return to History: The Breakup of the Soviet Union," *Brookings Review* 10 (Spring 1992): 30-33.

5. Ernest Gellner, *Nations and Nationalism* (Ithaca: Cornell University Press, 1983). Hans Kohn, *The Idea of Nationalism: A Study in Its Origin and Background* (New York: Macmillan, 1944).

6. Benedict Anderson, *Imagined Communities: Reflections on the Origins and Spread of Nationalism* (London: Verso Press, 1983).

7. Eugen J. Weber, *Peasants into Frenchmen: The Modernization of Rural France, 1870-1914* (Stanford, Calif.: Stanford University Press, 1976).

8. Eric Hobsbawm, who by no means is inclined to stress positive relationships between democracy and nationalism, also finds that "[t]he very act of democratizing politics, i.e., of turning subjects into citizens, tends to produce a populist consciousness which, seen in some lights, is hard to distinguish from a national, even a chauvinist, patriotism . . ." *Nations and Nationalism Since 1780: Programme, Myth, Reality* (Cambridge: Cambridge University Press, 1990), 88.

9. Gellner, op. cit., 55.

10. Fukuyama, op. cit., 201.

11. Ibid., 196-98.

12. Some aspects of this attitude are presented in my essay on "Humanism and Freedom," in Paul Peachey, John Kromkowski, George F. McLean, eds., *The Place of the Person in Social Life* (Washington, D.C.: Council for Research in Values and Philosophy, 1991), 33-43.

13. Fukuyama, op. cit., 266.

14. "Nationalism not only holds together the histories of the nineteenth and twentieth centuries, showing them to be part of a continuing crisis. It has also brought the histories of Asia, Africa, and the Pacific into relation with European history, making them part of a universal history." E. Kamenka, "Political Nationalism: The Evolution of the Idea," in E. Kamenka and J. Plamenatz, eds., *Nationalism: The Nature and Evolution of the Idea* (London: Edward Arnold, 1973), 3.

15. For example, "the Founding Fathers [of American democracy] thought that the liberty with which they were most concerned was menaced by democracy." Richard Hofstadter, *The American Political Tradition* (New York: Vintage Books, 1954), 10.

16. John Stuart Mill, *Considerations on Representative Government* (New York: Liberal Arts Press, 1958 [1861]), 230, 232-33.

17. Lord Acton, *Essays on Freedom and Power* (Boston: Beacon Press, 1948), 186.

18. "We must conclude that those states are substantially the most perfect which, like the British and Austrian Empires, include various distinct nationalities without oppressing them." Ibid., 193. "Inferior races are raised by living in political union with races intellectually superior." Ibid., 186.

19. Ibid., 168.

20. Lord Acton distinguished between bad (French) and good (British) doctrines of nationality: in the first case, state corresponds to nationality; in the second, nationality is derived from the state. Ibid., 183-84, 187. Anthony D. Smith makes a distinction between "territorial" and "ethnic" nations that corresponds to the difference between political and ethnic nationalism. *The Ethnic Origins of Nations* (Oxford: Basil Blackwell, 1986), 134-38.

21. Fukuyama, op. cit., 134-35.

22. Ibid., 216.

23. "Liberal democracies . . . are not self-sufficient: the community life on which they depend must ultimately come from a source different from liberalism itself." Ibid., 326. "Stable democracy requires a sometimes irrational democratic culture, and a spontaneous civil society growing out of preliberal traditions." Ibid., 334-35.

24. Avineri, op. cit., 30.

2.
COMMENTS ON
NATIONALISM & DEMOCRACY

Francis Fukuyama

Francis Fukuyama, the author of The End of History and the Last Man *(1992), is a resident consultant to the RAND Corporation in Washington, D.C., and a former deputy director of the policy planning staff of the U.S. State Department. This text is based upon remarks that he presented at a seminar at the National Endowment for Democracy on 3 June 1992.*

Ghia Nodia's essay is comprehensive, nuanced, and filled with insights large and small. Even though Nodia believes himself to be disagreeing with much that I have written, we actually concur about many things.

There are a number of points where we are in complete harmony: First, it is true that nationalism and democracy (understood as distinct from liberalism) are not mutually exclusive, but are in fact two sides of the same coin. This becomes evident if one looks at both phenomena from a historical or sociological perspective. In Western Europe, nationalism played a vital role in liberating various countries from monarchical absolutism in the eighteenth and nineteenth centuries. The Frankfurt Parliament of 1848 was equally German-nationalist and democratic, just as democratic and French-nationalist ideas were very strongly associated during the French Revolution. In our own day, nationalism is serving as an agent of liberation from communist dictatorship in a similar way.

When viewed sociologically, nationalism and democracy can be seen to have emerged out of the same process of industrialization. In this respect, Nodia may have misunderstood Ernest Gellner's observations about the relationship between nationalism and industrialization. Gellner did not mean to say that nationalism had a primarily economic function or represented the interests of certain economic actors; his point was that the economic process of industrialization created certain conditions under which nationalist ideas could flourish. Industrialization breaks down the old class lines typical of traditional agricultural societies, and necessitates the laying of a common linguistic and cultural groundwork upon which a national economy can be built. It is thus no accident that nationalism, in the modern sense of the word, did not exist prior to the Industrial Revolution. There was ethnicity, racial feeling, and the like, but not the belief that homogeneous cultural-linguistic groups should be organized into sovereign states. Democracy, similarly, springs out of that same historical process by which illiterate and inert peasants were turned into increasingly educated, urbanized workers.

"...many proponents of liberal democracy do not understand the ways in which moderate nationalism can contribute to the success of democracy as a matter of practical politics."

Nodia is also correct when he asserts that the major contradiction lies between nationalism and *liberalism*, rather than democracy. More precisely, liberalism combined with democracy implies the principle of universal recognition or universal individual rights. If, as I have argued elsewhere, liberalism is about the universal and equal recognition of every citizen's dignity as an autonomous human being, then the introduction of a national principle necessarily introduces distinctions between people. Persons who do not belong to the dominant nationality *ipso facto* have their dignity recognized in an inferior way to those who do belong—a flat contradiction of the principle of universal and equal recognition.

A further point on which we agree is that many proponents of liberal democracy do not understand the ways in which moderate nationalism can contribute to the success of democracy as a matter of practical politics. On an abstract level, the logical result of the principle of universal recognition is a universal homogeneous state where national borders disappear. (There is no reason, for example, why Canada and the United States should be separate countries.) But in the real world national distinctions do persist, and it is very hard to imagine stable democracies existing outside of these national contexts. In Western Europe, liberal democracies were constituted primarily within relatively homogeneous linguistic and cultural communities such as France, England, and later, in the twentieth century, Germany. Even in those developed, stable democracies, liberal democracy coexists with national identity, and national identity, despite the growing unification of the European Community, is at little risk of disappearing from Europe. It is really only in lands of new settlement, like the United States and Australia, that national identity can escape its ethnoracial aspect and become rooted in the principle of the liberal democratic regime itself. But in many other democracies like Japan or France this is not the case, and there is an intimate, continuing connection between democracy and a strong national identity.

Finally, I commend Nodia's rejection of the dogmatic liberal notion that all manifestations of nationalism are bad. As Nodia suggests, Mikhail Gorbachev has recently been a major promulgator of this particular idea. His use of it was, not surprisingly, quite self-serving: unless you kept the same old multiethnic USSR, of which he was the head, everything would lapse into chaos; hence there was no such thing as good nationalism. In fact, in the Soviet context nationalism was a necessary precondition for the emergence of democracy in the successor republics. The old Soviet Union had to break up along national lines before any kind of genuine democratic revolution could begin.

Now for my disagreements with Nodia. On a more theoretical level, he argues that the liberal principle of universal recognition, based on a kind of universal equality of rights, has no inherently greater rationality than the national principle. He correctly attributes to me the view that universal recognition is rational because it is based on a fundamental distinction between that which is human and that which is nonhuman. That is to say, human beings intrinsically possess a certain quality that distinguishes them from nonhuman nature—it can be either their superior reason, as it was for the ancients; the capacity for autonomous choice, as in the Christian (and later the German-idealist) tradition; or perhaps some combination of the two, as in some other accounts. But it is the existence of a basic distinction separating man from the animals and the rest of lower creation that rightfully gives man dominion over nature. This also means that all human beings are fundamentally the same with regard to that distinction, and are thus equal in this most decisive respect.

Nodia notes, quite correctly, that the philosophical basis for believing that there is a fundamental distinction between human and nonhuman is today quite uncertain, and that this distinction has been under attack for some time in the West. A recent example is Václav Havel's essay in connection with the Rio Summit on the global environment, published in the *New York Times* of 3 June 1992, in which he questions the whole project of man's domination over nature, and whether man in fact has a superior dignity that gives him the right to do this sort of thing. The environmental movement today has become the leading promulgator of the idea that there is really no rational basis for the distinction between human and nonhuman nature.

It is also true, as Nodia emphasizes, that people live in national communities and that to most people distinctions between Frenchmen and Germans or between Serbs and Croats are much more vivid and important than the distinction between humanity as such and something that is not human. Nonetheless, I think that we must ask whether the modern tendency to deny the reasonableness of the distinction between the human and nonhuman is something we should celebrate, or rather something we should resist. For if we abandon the principle of superior *human* dignity in favor of a principle of *national* dignity, we lay the groundwork for two seemingly contradictory outcomes. On the one hand, there will be a *particularization* of rights that will throw into question the liberal democratic principle of human equality. And on the other hand, we open the door to a *superuniversalization* of rights that will invest nonhuman nature with rights. The ultimate effect of this will be to delegitimize the entire project of conquering nature, including the industrialization process and the economic growth that flows from it.

> *"Nationalism can coexist quite well with liberalism as long as the former becomes tolerant. That is to say, national identity has to be pushed off into the realm of private life and culture...."*

There is a second respect in which universal recognition has a claim to superior rationality over the national principle. To put it in Kantian terms, if all people desire recognition of their intrinsic worth as persons, then universal equal recognition is the only possible rule of practical reason that can adjudicate all individual claims for the recognition of human dignity in a manner that does not satisfy some people's dignity at the expense of others. Such a rule of reason would apply, as Kant says, to all rational beings, regardless of whether they are human or not. We need no empirical knowledge about these beings for the rule to remain a rational one. In more practical terms, the problematic character of most nationalist regimes becomes apparent if one considers how the dignity of people outside the dominant national group is recognized, or whether it really can be adequately recognized if the regime in principle asserts a distinction between one *ethnos* and another.

On a practical level, of course, liberal democracy and nationalism have found ways of coexisting rather peacefully. The terrible experiences of the 1930s and World War II seem to have implanted in us a tendency to think that nationalism must inevitably degenerate into fascism, but that is simply not the case. Nationalism can coexist quite well with liberalism as long as the former becomes tolerant. That is to say, national identity has to be pushed off into the realm of private life and culture, rather than being politicized and made the basis of legal rights. Alternatively, national pride can be sublimated into economic competition, as in the case of Japanese supercomputers. Nationalism can become tolerant if national identity or national culture is something that is fundamentally open to other people, so that an African can become a Frenchman if he speaks French and likes brie and adopts the other manners and mores that give coherence to traditional French culture.

It is necessary to inject a note of caution here, however, for the coexistence between the national and liberal principles will always remain uneasy. For one thing, that coexistence works best in racially and culturally homogeneous countries where the dominant culture is relatively secure, or in lands of new settlement where the culture is primarily political rather than ethnic in nature. Current fears about immigration in Western Europe demonstrate the limits of this compatibility. There are many Germans, for example, who very much doubt that an African can become a German just by speaking German and adopting various habits and trappings of German culture.

In the postcommunist East, the coexistence of the national and liberal principles is even more problematic because there are very few homogeneous nation-states like France or England. In fact, most states in the region are rough ethnic patchworks where there is no single clearly dominant culture. Unless political authorities define "nation" in the most abstract and formal way, there will always be a problem of the rights of ethnolinguistic minorities. To take a practical example: if the Ukrainians continue to define citizenship rights and educational policies in the tolerant terms that they have initially chosen, using a territorial definition of nationality that confers full citizenship on anyone living within the borders of Ukraine, then their country can survive. If, however, Ukrainian parentage or language or other aspects of Ukrainian ethnocultural identity become preconditions for citizenship or other kinds of rights, then I think that the country will explode as Russians and other minority nationalities rebel against domination by ethnic Ukrainians.

One solution to this problem is the establishment of group rights of the sort found in Lebanon. Yet as the example of Lebanon suggests, this is not in the end a very satisfactory solution. Adopting the principle of group rights raises hard questions about what constitutes a legitimate group, who belongs to what group, when to take a census to find out how many people belong to which groups, who is to decide these issues, and so on. Thus one is ultimately driven back to the Kantian view that the only rational form of recognition is the impartial recognition of people as individual human beings rather than as members of this or that particular national group.

There is one final point. Nodia sometimes appears to treat nationalism primarily as a transitional strategy. Let us not castigate nationalism, he argues, for it is a useful means of getting to liberal democracy, particularly in posttotalitarian parts of the world like the former Soviet Union. But his analysis as a whole raises a larger philosophical question, and it is not clear how he means to answer it: Is there something in the national principle that is ultimately superior to the principle of universal recognition that underlies liberal democracy? That is to say, it is perfectly possible to see how, for countries like Ukraine or Russia, nationalism can prove a useful, if dangerous, aid for getting through this difficult period following the downfall of communism. But is there any reason to think that in the end, when democratic stability and prosperity are achieved, people are going to find it more satisfying to live in nationally defined political entities than in liberal ones that recognize only one's formal, abstract humanity?

The best test case of this in the world right now is Quebec, rather than any of the cases in the former Soviet Union. This is because Quebec is a subdivision within a prosperous and stable liberal democratic country. And yet for certain Québécois, the universal liberal identity conferred on them by Canadian citizenship in *une province comme les autres* is somehow just not enough. The breakup of Canada along national lines would be an interesting piece of evidence concerning the adequacy of modern liberal democracy. But be that as it may, it remains unclear to me whether Nodia regards nationalism merely as a midwife to the birth and development of democracy, or as an indispensable element of even the most advanced stages of liberal democracy.

Shlomo Avineri

Shlomo Avineri, *professor of political science at the Hebrew University of Jerusalem, was recently a guest scholar at the Brookings Institution, where he worked on problems of nationalism in Eastern Europe. His books include* The Social and Political Thought of Karl Marx *(1968),* Hegel's Theory of the Modern State *(1973),* The Making of Modern Zionism *(1981), and* Communitarianism and Individualism *(with Avner de Shalit, 1992).*

Ghia Nodia's perceptive essay on nationalism and democracy brings out most clearly the ambivalent role that nationalism plays in the project of modernity. Far from being a primordial or irrational residue of traditional societies, nationalism as a political force (as distinct from mere ethnicity) is a profoundly modern phenomenon. As Nodia shows, it is inextricably bound up with the French Revolutionary tradition of popular sovereignty, as well as the Kantian doctrine of human personality and autonomy. Liberals who view nationalism as an atavism are as wrong as the orthodox Marxists who, beguiled by their master's dictum that "proletarians have no fatherland," tried to consign nationalism to the dustbin of history. As current developments show, national issues have become dominant in the political discourse of the postcommunist East.

This is evidenced not only by the violent eruptions in Bosnia, Croatia, Moldova, Georgia, and Nagorno-Karabakh, but also by the abysmal way that the newly independent Baltic states have been treating their Russian and Polish minorities, by the breakup of the Czech and Slovak Federative Republic, and by dozens of other flashpoints of actual or potential ethnic strife. The list could be augmented by the threat hanging over the future of the 25 million ethnic Russians who live outside of Russia; the problems of Hungarian minorities in Slovakia, Romania, and the former Yugoslavia; and the predicament of areas like the Kaliningrad oblast (formerly Königsberg in East Prussia), which is now part of Russia but is cut off from that republic by Lithuania and Belarus.

Anyone who believed that postcommunist political discourse would concentrate mainly on the issues of democratization and the development of market economies now knows better. Nodia rightly distinguishes between the liberal and the democratic ingredients that make up Western liberal democracies, and explains why the communist legacy has given an antiliberal version of nationalism a good chance of gaining ascendancy in many postcommunist societies. Leninist policies, followed also by Tito, gave territorial expression to national-linguistic entities and thus even dictated the form in which both the Soviet Union and Yugoslavia would break up into discrete states, each burdened with numerous questions regarding national minorities and potentially contestable borders.

I agree with most of Nodia's vindication of nationalism in the context of modernity, but there are a few nuances that I would like to underline. A major reason why nationalism seems to run contrary to the universalist norms of liberal political theory has to do with the historic irony that so much of the work of formulating and disseminating universalist values was done under the political and intellectual hegemony of two specific cultures: the French and the English. In the light of the ideas of human rights popularized by the French Revolution, or the political liberalism and market economics spread through the dominance of England and later the United States, nationalism appeared as particularistic, petty, divisive, retrograde, and a deviation from universality. What are Breton folkways as compared to the riches of French culture and its glorious *mission civilisatrice*? What are the Gaelic-speaking communities of the British Isles' "Celtic fringe" if not an anachronism at the margin of the mighty English-speaking world culture? France and the English-speaking powers trumpeted, each in its own way, the victory of an ecumenical culture claiming a basis in rationality and universally shared values. They then elevated these historical cultures to the level of a truly catholic norm, and woe betide the Irish, the Zionists, or other peoples whose smaller-scale loyalties made them appear parochial, inward-looking, obscurantist, xenophobic, ethnocentric, or (worst of all) premodern.

In other words, this abstract universalism—which was nothing else than a hypostasis of a given, historical set of cultures—declared itself to be the sole norm of historical progress (even occasionally enthroning itself as the "end of history"), and then looked down on the cultures of small nations as both provincial and pernicious. At bottom, it was yet another example of the cultural imperialism of Great Nations—large ethnolinguistic groups that preach universalism and see in their own assimilationist, triumphalist progress the inevitable unfolding of Reason in History. They are prone to dismiss as retrograde the *cri de coeur* of the small nations upon which they press with the massive weight of their economic, political, military, and ideological power. In the former Soviet Union, a similar Great-Nation sense of self-assurance was inherited from the Czarist tradition: Russification, it was thought, meant the spread of civilization and culture.

> "It is the Great-Nation blindness to the strength of nationalism that has made so many observers oblivious to the nationalist potential in the postcommunist world."

As Nodia points out, the need to belong to a community (and not just some aggregate of individuals) is part of human personality. Members of large linguistic and cultural groups take this as a given to such a degree that they associate their own culture with culture as such, and hence sometimes cannot even understand what it means to be deprived of it. As Adam Mickiewicz says when addressing his homeland in the opening stanzas of *Pan Tadeusz*: "You are like health/Only he who has lost it knows what it is." Or as another Polish thinker, Leszek Kolakowski, once remarked, the nation or the tribe is an experience, while humanity is an aspiration. It is the Great-Nation blindness to the strength of nationalism that has made so many observers oblivious to the nationalist potential in the postcommunist world.

To this we must add the realization that many postcommunist societies are now coming out of a time warp of 75 or 45 years. This does not mean, of course, that "nothing has happened" there, or that with communism gone, these societies will return to where they were before 1917 or 1945: you cannot step twice into the same river. But it does mean that postcommunist societies live in a kind of temporal dissonance. Economically, for example, many of them are highly industrialized societies—but without a market. Politically, they have been highly politicized and highly mobilized—but have no experience with the politics of democratic mobilization. Nodia rightly points out that transitions in postcommunist societies differ from transitions in premodern Third World countries: the former are not transitions *to* modernity, but transitions *from* a "deviant" kind of modernity toward what is considered "normal" modernity in the Western sense.

When it comes to nationalism, this means that issues which most Western societies settled through trial and error, accommodation, or drastic forced adjustment following World War II, are still open questions that the people of Eastern Europe must grapple with even as the countries of the West move on to other, presumably "postmodern" discourses (the environment, gender issues, etc.). While demands for cultural autonomy continue to remain unresolved in the West, the conflicts that they engender do not, as a rule, threaten the whole fabric of the body politic. Britain's failure to end the strife in Northern Ireland, for instance, does not pose a mortal threat to the British polity and its democratic structures. Eastern Europe, on the other hand, still lives in 1939 or perhaps 1914: its political discourse is somehow "retarded" and out of joint, in the sense that the institutionalized solutions offered by the Western nation-state are not yet viable in the East. History there has in a sense been "arrested," and political discourse seems to echo a time long past in the West.

Nodia is again right in pointing to the Janus-like nature of nationalism with regard to liberal values: it has its universalist, harmonistic version (the Mazzini mode, if you like) and its exclusivist, aggressive variant (the Treitschke mode). It is to be feared that economic hardships plus the failure of democratic reform may push some postcommunist societies into the latter, more dangerous mode.

Practically all postcommunist societies have ethnic minorities, and in many cases, as in the ex-Soviet Union, borders reflect the whims and fiats of the old rulers and have little to do with either history or linguistic delineations. To imagine that in all cases these problems can be settled peacefully and without changing existing boundaries would be to stretch credulity to its limits. It is here that the precommunist historical traditions of the societies involved become relevant. No universal code applies to all, and anyone who wants to know whether a given society will go about solving its problems amicably or violently would do better to look to historical and national traditions rather than to quantitative data concerning economic development, GNP figures, and the like. It is in this sense as well that history is returning; patronizing Western liberal talk about "Balkanization" is another example of the cultural hegemonism and imperialism mentioned earlier.

Paradoxically, one of the few positive aspects of Soviet hegemony—achieved at a terrible and totally unjustifiable cost—was the Pax Sovietica that the USSR enforced in Eastern Europe and the old Czarist empire. From the end of the civil war period in Russia and from 1945 in Eastern Europe, no full-blown ethnic war was allowed to break out in that part of the world, which for centuries had been a crucible of clashing nationalisms. Communism sought to impose its version of modernity on nationalism, trying to mold it according to its own (admittedly flawed) understanding of the Enlightenment project. The failure of the Marxist-Leninist interpretation of modernity signals that the time is ripe to give liberal democracy a try. But it will take more than snide dismissals of nationalism—especially if they come from cultures that take their own stable national identity for granted—to exorcise the demons of hate and anger that fuel ethnic strife in the postcommunist world.

II.
The Challenge of Ethnic Conflict

3.
DEMOCRACY IN DIVIDED SOCIETIES

Donald L. Horowitz

Donald L. Horowitz is the Charles S. Murphy Professor of Law and Professor of Political Science at Duke University. He is the author of Ethnic Groups in Conflict *(1985) and* A Democratic South Africa? Constitutional Engineering in a Divided Society *(1991) and coeditor of* Immigrants in Two Democracies: French and American Experience *(1992), among other books. An earlier version of this article was presented to the Aspen Institute Strategy Group.*

Democratization is a worldwide movement, but it is neither universal nor uniformly successful where it has begun. Some authoritarian or semidemocratic states may be untouched by the democratic movement; others may find ways to thwart the movement at the outset; still others may move along a democratic path, only to have the changes aborted. There are many reasons, of course, why democratization and democracies may fail, among them the resistance of entrenched civilian or military elites, the absence of conducive social or cultural conditions, and inaptly designed institutions. In many countries of Africa, Asia, Eastern Europe, and the former Soviet Union, a major reason for the failure of democratization is ethnic conflict.

Democracy is about inclusion and exclusion, about access to power, about the privileges that go with inclusion and the penalties that accompany exclusion. In severely divided societies, ethnic identity provides clear lines to determine who will be included and who will be excluded. Since the lines appear unalterable, being in and being out may quickly come to look permanent. In ethnic politics, inclusion may affect the distribution of important material and nonmaterial goods, including the prestige of the various ethnic groups and the identity of the state as belonging more to one group than another. Again and again in divided societies, there is a tendency to conflate inclusion in the government with inclusion in the community and exclusion from government with exclusion from the community.

Ethnically divided societies thus have a special version of the usual
democratic problem of assuring decent treatment of the opposition.
Opposition to government is always susceptible of portrayal as resistance
to the popular will. An ethnically differentiated opposition can easily be
depicted as consisting of particularly dangerous enemies: historical
enemies, enemies who do not accept the current identity of the state,
enemies who are plotting to break up the state or to steal it for their
own group—as indeed they may be, given the crucial importance of
state power and the costs of exclusion from it.

Where ethnic relations undergo significant improvements during an
authoritarian period, that is very likely to improve the prospects for
democracy. Relations between Thais and Chinese in Thailand and
between Mainlanders and Taiwanese on Taiwan were hostile and even
violent after World War II. Several decades later, those relations were
far less prone to conflict, and rates of intermarriage were higher than
is typical of deeply divided societies. These changes facilitated
democratization in both countries, because they reduced the fear that
each group had of the other. At the other extreme, most African
countries remain severely divided, and ethnic divisions have proved a
major impediment to the attainment of stable democracy all over the
continent.

Democracy has progressed furthest in those East European countries
that have the fewest serious ethnic cleavages (Hungary, the Czech
Republic, and Poland) and progressed more slowly or not at all in those
that are deeply divided (Slovakia, Bulgaria, Romania, and of course the
former Yugoslavia). It is true that the first group of states was more
prosperous, had at least some democratic traditions, and had closer ties
to the West. But there is also a direct relationship between ethnic
conflict and nondemocratic development in the second group. The use
of ethnic hostility by former communists in Serbia, Croatia, and Bosnia
to support ethnically exclusive regimes and authoritarian tendencies is
well known. The heavy-handed Slovak regime of former communist
Vladimír Mečiar is hardly comparable to the regimes in Croatia and
Serbia, but it does have a record of attempting to control the press,
pack the Constitutional Court, and limit the language rights of
Hungarians in the south of the country. The democratic movement in
Romania, which received its strongest impetus in multiethnic
Transylvania, was quickly transformed into a narrower Romanian
nationalism, occasionally inclined to xenophobia, especially fearful of the
Hungarian minority, and conducive to the continued governmental role
of former communists. In Bulgaria, an anticommunist parliamentary
plurality, attentive to popular fears of the Turkish minority (and of other
Muslims), was unable to form a stable government by coalescing with
the Turkish party. When the government lost a vote of confidence, it
was succeeded by a party of ex-communists who had led the anti-

Turkish agitation and who then embarked on a series of purges of the administration and the press. Ethnic conflict has fed authoritarian tendencies in Eastern Europe, as it has elsewhere.

Although it is widely recognized that ethnic conflict makes both the initiation of democratization and the practice of democracy difficult, the nature of the difficulties, especially the extent to which they are structurally embedded and not readily amenable to sheer exercises of good will, is rarely specified. Ethnicity poses obstacles at the threshold of democratization and obstacles after the threshold is crossed. In a variety of ways, direct and indirect, ethnic conflict can be conducive to authoritarianism, and, in at least equally various ways, democracy can facilitate either majority rule and the exclusion of minorities or minority rule and the exclusion of majorities. None of this is to say that nothing can be done and that fatalism is the appropriate response. Things can be done—for some deeply divided societies are relatively democratic—but there are good systemic reasons why it is difficult to produce institutions conducive to the emergence of multiethnic democracy.

Before laying out the difficulties, perhaps it is best to make clear that severely divided societies lie at one end of a spectrum. At the other end are fluid societies that have long contained groups whose descendants have blended into the general population (various immigrants in the United States and in France) or whose interactions have been at relatively low levels of conflict (English, Welsh, Scots, and Irish in Britain and Australia). In the middle is a category of more severely divided societies, where groups have strongly held political aspirations and interact as groups but where several favorable conditions have moderated the effects of ethnic conflict. In these countries, external forces have historically tended to foster internal integration; several other cleavages (religion, class, often region) compete for attention with ethnicity and are reflected in the party system; and ethnic issues emerged late in relation to other cleavages and to the development of parties, so that party politics is not a perfect reflection of ethnic conflict. Among these countries are Switzerland, Canada, and Belgium—all, significantly, federations. It is difficult to generalize from these structurally advantaged countries to severely divided societies, such as Northern Ireland or Sri Lanka, where the issue of birth identity does not alternate with others, where external forces are neutral or disintegrative, and where parties reflect the ethnic cleavage. In such countries, democracy is always difficult.

Obstacles at the Threshold

Before democratization can proceed, the old regime must either agree or be forced to change; or, if it is defeated, the victors must agree among themselves to a democratic dispensation. In many severely divided societies, these conditions cannot be met. The delicacy of the ethnic issue may combine with an established leadership's contentment with the status quo to induce that leadership to pass up opportunities to democratize. Even opponents of the leadership may sense the possibility of worse alternatives to the status quo, some of which may be precipitated by democratization. Alternatively, an ethnically exclusive regime may resist a change that will bring its ethnic opponents to power by democratic processes. If a new beginning is brought about as a result of ethnic insurgency, democracy may be aborted as some ethnic contenders sense that others will have the advantage in a democratic regime.

It may seem curious that movements for further democratization have largely bypassed some semidemocratic or semiauthoritarian states in Southeast Asia. Yet these delicately balanced regimes, more democratic in the case of Malaysia, less in Singapore and Indonesia, are cases in which popular discontent is not at the same levels that were reached in Thailand, Burma, and the Philippines. Despite ethnic favoritism, the question of inclusion and exclusion is somewhat blurred in the former set of countries, and the regimes themselves would be firmly opposed to further democratization. Even at the height of the worldwide democratization movement, the question was hardly raised in Malaysia, Singapore, and Indonesia—which is testimony to the ability of partial satisfaction (a sense that ethnic exclusion could be much worse) coupled with regime strength to preempt change.

More sharply exclusive regimes generally need to be more active if they are to thwart change. Ethnically exclusive regimes come in two general varieties: bifurcated polities, in which roughly half or more than half the state rules the rest; and minority-dominated polities, in which the base of a regime has progressively narrowed, particularly after the end of competitive elections, so that one or two small groups rule the majority. In either case, there is likely to be resistance to any change that might bring ethnic opponents to power.

Bifurcated regimes often have unpleasant memories of elections, for the parties of their ethnic opponents may have won them. Accordingly, there is little inclination to facilitate a recurrence. Togo and the Congo Republic both have northern regimes (based, respectively, on the Kabrai and the Mbochi) that came to power after military coups reversed the ethnic results of elections. Neither regime has had a special desire to accommodate a democratic process it identified with its southern (Ewe or Lari) opponents. Consequently, both took steps to disrupt the process.[1]

More narrowly based regimes willing to use draconian methods—Zaire, for example—have also been able to thwart democratization. Most others have resorted to manipulating the process.

Kenya, with its Kalenjin-dominated minority government, finally succumbed to Western pressure and conducted a multiparty election. But the incumbent president, Daniel arap Moi, was able to use a combination of intimidation, violence, and ethnic divisions among the opposition to win both the presidency and a parliamentary majority on a plurality of votes, mainly from his own group and several other small ethnic groups. The result is a regime that continues to exclude the two largest groups, Kikuyu and Luo. Likewise, Cameroon's President Paul Biya, presiding over a government supported mainly by Beti and Bulu and opposed by all the rest, benefited from an opposition divided along ethnic lines and an election boycott by a major party. Biya put together a legislative coalition in which his party is dominant, and he won a plurality in a presidential election. Thereafter, he arrested his main opponent. The same narrowly composed authoritarian government thus continues to rule. In a dubiously conducted election in Ghana, the military ruler, Jerry Rawlings, won the presidency, supported by 93 percent of the vote in his own Ewe-dominated area, but polling less than one-third in Ashanti, thus reviving an earlier polarization.

Manipulation does not succeed everywhere. In Benin and Zambia, narrow regimes yielded to popular pressure for free elections, which they then lost. These, however, are the exceptional cases, and, as we shall see, what they gave way to cannot be characterized as multiethnic democracy.

A great many armed insurrections are aimed against ethnically-based regimes. Where they have not succeeded militarily, they have also generally provoked countermeasures, reducing rather than enhancing democratic prospects. That has been true in Sri Lanka and Sudan; certainly, the minority insurgencies in Burma are among the main reasons the regime fears democratization. Even if the insurgents win or at least win sufficiently to force concessions, the results can still be disappointing for democrats. In Liberia and Somalia, the victory of the insurgents produced only further ethnic violence and warfare. In Zimbabwe, the victory of the Patriotic Front, which led to independence, then generated warfare by Robert Mugabe's Shona-led regime against Joshua Nkomo's Ndebele opposition, until Nkomo capitulated to the one-party state. The Afghan civil war has produced something like a de facto Tajik and Uzbek state in the north and a Pushtun state in the south, neither with democratic inclinations. A similar result may follow ultimately in Tajikistan, where ethnically differentiated forces have been fighting since shortly after the dissolution of the Soviet Union. Insurgency is not conducive to the establishment of democratic institutions.

Even under the most favorable conditions, the defeat of authoritarian regimes on the battlefield does not mean that the victorious insurgents will be able to make a democratic transition in a divided society. Those favorable conditions were certainly present in Ethiopia. Tolerant, democratic inclinations were in evidence. Two of the three major insurgent groups, Tigrayans and Oromo, had agreed that the third, Eritreans, were entitled to their own separate state. For the rest, the new rulers in Addis Ababa had planned a democratic Ethiopia that would accord considerable autonomy to the remaining ethnic groups. But then the Oromo leaders accused their Tigrayan former partners of attempting to rig the 1992 regional elections. The Oromo, the most numerous ethnic group in the country, proceeded to begin a new insurgency.[2] Their withdrawal created a *fait accompli*: over 90 percent of the seats were won by the Tigrayan party and its allies. With Tigrayans dominant in the armed forces, Ethiopia, conquered by a broad-based insurgency, is ruled by a relatively small minority. As we shall see, similar results can be achieved without insurgency.

Narrowing the Boundaries of Community

The problems of inclusion and exclusion do not disappear when new institutions are being adopted and put into operation. At these points, conceptions of the scope of the political community will limit the participation of some groups in the institutions of the new regime.

One of the ironies of democratic development is that, as the future is being planned, the past intrudes with increasing severity. In this field, there is no such thing as a fresh start. In ethnic relations, history often leads to exclusive conceptions of community. Take the question of who belongs here. The answer usually turns on who is thought to have arrived here first and where "here" actually is. Those who think their ancestors arrived earlier are likely to demand political priority by virtue of indigenousness over those deemed to be immigrants. Similarly, it is common to demand that a given territory be considered part of one "world," rather than part of another nearby. The implication is that those inhabitants who are identified with the "world" in which the territory is properly located have priority over those who are not so identified.

Asia is full of such claims: that the Sri Lankan Tamils really belong to South India, that the Bengalis are illegitimately in Assam, that the Southeast Asian Chinese are immigrants, that the Muslim Arakanese in Burma are actually Bangladeshis, that the Mohajirs in Karachi are not proper Sindhis. In Eastern Europe, questions of belonging are highly charged with historical memory. Two of the largest minorities—Hungarians and Turkish and other Muslims—are thought to be present only as relics of a Hapsburg or Ottoman domination that for centuries repressed those who are now tempted to exclude them in turn. The former Soviet Union has a special variant of these struggles over belonging. Not only are the Russians and other Slavs who migrated to non-Slavic republics considered to be settlers identified with a discredited imperial regime, but some of the areas in which they often form majorities lie outside Russia only because of territorial boundaries constructed by the Soviet regime on grounds increasingly regarded by Russians as capricious and therefore alterable. As a result, the attempts of Moldovans, Kazakhs, or Estonians to exclude Russians from the community can be met with Russian efforts to detach territory from the excluding state.

In Moldova, the less-than-two-thirds of the population that speaks Romanian managed to declare their language the official language of the new republic. The assumption, understood as such by Russian, Gagauz, and Ukrainian minorities, especially in the Trans-Dniester, is that Moldova is for Moldovans.[3] Much of Moldova was taken by Stalin from Romania in 1940 and incorporated in the Soviet Union. But Trans-Dniester was not part of the pre-1940 Romanian territory; it was instead split off from the Ukraine. Most of its Russian population settled there after 1940. To Romanian-speakers, the recency of the Slavic immigration compounds the illegitimacy of the settlers' claims. To Trans-Dniestrians, the illegitimate amalgamation of the two lands in 1940 means that their territory does not belong to Moldova. The claim to have arrived here first is thus countered by the claim that here is not here at all.

These underlying issues of the social and territorial boundaries of the community surface in the construction of new democracies. If the regime on Taiwan were still seriously considered to be simply the locus of the mainland government in exile, it would be illegitimate to have it ruled by Taiwanese; if, on the other hand, Mainlanders were still considered to be merely sojourners, their continued participation at the center of power would be in question. The fact that both of these questions of where and who have more or less been resolved has greatly facilitated multiethnic democratization on Taiwan. Comparable questions have not been resolved between Lithuanians and Poles in Lithuania, between Kazakhs and Russians in Kazakhstan, or among Georgians, Abkhazians, and South Ossetians in Georgia. The migration of Russians to republics along the European, Central Asian, and Siberian periphery of the former Soviet Union has given rise to a great many measures to treat them as less than full members of the community: violence in Tuva, settlement restrictions in Yakutia, weighted voting in Tatarstan, restrictive citizenship in several republics. In Latvia and Estonia, both with large Russian minorities, substantial bodies of opinion at independence favored the repatriation of Russian settlers; in Estonia, the citizenship law disfranchised 42 percent of the population.

The boundary of the political community is an issue that manifests itself in the answer to three questions: Who is a citizen? Among citizens, who has what privileges? Whose norms and practices are symbolically aligned with those of the state? Beyond admission to citizenship, then, there is the question of special provision for the admission of one group more than another to educational institutions, to the civil service, or to the armed forces. Where belonging is contested, special provision is an indicator of political priority. And so is a language law that makes Georgian the official language of Georgia or Kazakh the official language of Kazakhstan, displacing competing languages. These policies symbolize the priority of the group speaking the official language, and they reflect restrictive conceptions of indigenousness. In the case of Georgia, they are the outcome of long disputes over whether Georgians or Abkhazians arrived in the territory first and whether all groups that arrived in Georgia after 1801—allegedly, Ossetians and Azeris did—ought simply to be dispossessed.[4]

The Georgian case makes clear some of the connections between ethnic conflict and authoritarian rule. The more deeply the post-Soviet regime became mired in policies designed to exclude minorities, the more autocratic it became as well. Extreme forms of ethnic exclusion require a legal framework that is ultimately inimical to democratic principles. They make it impossible to apply uniform conceptions of representation or to treat like cases alike. If, in addition, the excluded groups adopt unlawful methods of protest, there is likely to be a spate of statutes and regulations authorizing arbitrary arrest and search, detention without trial, and restrictions on freedom of expression. Political leaders who advocate ethnically extremist positions are also more inclined than ethnic moderates are to support authoritarian measures.[5] This is another way in which the pursuit of ethnic conflict is likely to foster authoritarianism.

Inclusion and Exclusion

There is yet a further obstacle to constructing a democratic multiethnic community after the process of democratization has begun in a severely divided society. This obstacle does not derive from such overtly restrictive conceptions of community as those based on indigenousness. Rather, it derives from the inherent difficulty any regime has in maintaining the inclusiveness of a polity superimposed on an ethnically divided society. Africa has relatively few claims to group priority by virtue of indigenousness, but it is nevertheless suffused with problems of ethnic inclusion and exclusion.

Zambia was widely regarded as a major African success in democratization, largely because the incumbent president, Kenneth Kaunda, reluctantly acceded to free elections, did not rig them, and conceded defeat when he lost. Such an assessment, however, supremely exalts form over substance, for neither the outgoing nor the incoming regime has had the ability to keep all the major groups included. In fact, the new regime has begun to repeat the very same process of exclusion that narrowed the base of its predecessor.

Like Frederick Chiluba, the winner of the 1991 election, Kaunda had earlier acquired power (in his case, from the British) at the head of a party with broad multiethnic support. Of the half-dozen major groups, none of them comprising more than a fifth of the population, only the Ila and the Tonga in the south supported the opposition. Soon after independence, however, ethnic factions arose within the ruling party. After they were defeated in party elections, Lozi leaders joined the opposition. At this point, Kaunda took defensive measures to counter the alleged overrepresentation of Bemba in the party leadership. Discontented Bemba, who believed they had played a leading role in the independence struggle, then formed their own party. As the opposition grew, the ethnic scope of the ruling party contracted, until Kaunda declared a single-party state that simultaneously ended the electoral threat to his rule and disguised the narrow base of his party, confined by then largely to the Nyanja of the east. When elections finally were held, nearly two decades later, Kaunda won all of the seats in the Eastern Province and only a handful elsewhere. An interethnic opposition, the Movement for Multiparty Democracy (MMD), won the rest in a landslide.

> *"In each case, victory marked the beginning of an ethnic struggle, in which group leaders contended for the domination of the new regime and peeled away from the multiethnic party as they were defeated."*

In little more than a year, the cycle began again. Claims were made that Bemba had received an unfair share of government and party appointments; a Lozi and a Bemba minister were sacked; another Lozi and an influential Ila minister resigned. A new Bemba-based party was formed. Several regions were being organized against the government. By early 1993, the regime declared a state of emergency, citing a plot allegedly involving members of Kaunda's family. The former, broad-based opposition was well on the way to replicating Kaunda's minority-dominated, authoritarian regime.

Quite clearly, the breadth of the MMD's multiethnic support against Kaunda at the time of the 1991 election was a function of the transitory nature of the contest in which it was engaged, just as Kaunda's own initial support against the colonial regime did not long survive the departure of the British. In each case, victory marked the beginning of an ethnic struggle, in which group leaders contended for the domination of the new regime and peeled away from the multiethnic party as they were defeated. Such parties, left with minority support after the postindependence struggles, typically outlawed the opposition, declared a single-party state, pronounced the single party to be ethnically inclusive, but in fact kept power in the hands of minorities that could not have kept it had elections continued to be held. This was true not only for Zambia, but for Kenya, Cameroon, Uganda, Chad, the Ivory Coast, Guinea, Mauritania, and Sierra Leone, among others. In each case, the single party was a mask for ethnic domination.[6] If events in Zambia now seem to be following a similar course, that is because the same forces and the same dynamics are present. Why should they have changed merely because new elections were held?

What drives the cyclical processes of inclusion and exclusion is the changing context. It is not difficult to conclude that the colonial regime, or the Kaunda regime, or the Moi regime is ethnically exclusive and undemocratic. Even that is no guarantee that those who oppose it will unite at the polls, as Moi's victory in Kenya and Biya's in Cameroon show. Even if opponents do unite, that is not because they have suppressed their differences, but because those differences are not yet relevant. They become relevant only when it is time to decide who will rule. At that point, the question of group desert comes into play: the Nyanja are better educated and thus qualified to rule; the Bemba were more committed to ousting the former regime; the Lozi have been denied the regional autonomy promised them at independence. Each of these claims produces a hostile answer from others.

Now it is perfectly understandable that a party that wins three-quarters or more of the votes cast in a general election, as the Zambian MMD did in 1991,[7] may face a problem of distribution: it has too many supporters—or, rather, the old regime had too many opponents—and some of them will soon be disappointed. But, once the disaffection begins, why were Kaunda and others in his position unable to brake the slide, in order to end up with a diminished majority rather than the narrow minority regimes with which they were ultimately saddled?

The answer is that some regimes are able to stop at a point at which roughly half the state's ethnic groups are pitted against the other half. These are the states in which affinities among groups produce the bifurcation of north against south, or of Christians against Muslims, or of one core group against others, such as Mbochi against Lari in the Congo or Kabrai against Ewe in Togo. Where such obvious affinities and disparities are present, the resulting bifurcation often produces severe polarization and conflict. This polarization generally results in a narrow election victory, in which nearly half the state feels excluded and from which it may call upon the military to deliver it. This is roughly the history of Nigerian politics that led to the coups of 1966 and the Biafran war of 1967 to 1970. But such bifurcating affinities and disparities are not always present, and it may then become difficult to stop the slide toward minority rule of the sort represented by Zambia and Cameroon. Moreover, if the rulers of a regime can convince themselves, by proclaiming a one-party state or by some other means, that they will not have to face a free choice of the electorate again, the narrowness of the regime is a great distributive advantage: there are fewer claimants for what the state offers. Eventually, however, excluded majorities may feel the need to take up arms against the regime, as they did against Idi Amin's minority regime in Uganda and as they have periodically done against Hafez al-Assad's in Syria.

When democratic elections produce ethnic exclusion, undemocratic reactions to it can be expected. In Benin, like Zambia touted as a model of redemocratization, the 1991 elections brought out the same three-way ethnic rivalry that had manifested itself after independence. Each of the three main presidential candidates received between 70 and 80 percent of his first-round support from his home region. In the French-style runoff, this was compressed into a north-south struggle, in which the victorious candidate won nearly 90 percent of the southern vote and the defeated candidate won nearly 94 percent of the northern vote. A year later, northern-dominated army units attempted a coup and then a mutiny, as they had done with greater success decades earlier, the last time an exclusively southern government came to power. The extent to which military rule in Africa is a function of the ethnic failures of electoral politics can hardly be overestimated. The current round of elections is no more secure against those failures than the earlier, postcolonial round was.

Democratic Institutions and Undemocratic Results

As the example of the Benin presidential runoff suggests, political institutions and decision rules can make a major difference in ethnic outcomes. The Benin runoff converted a tripolar contest into a bipolar one. The federalism of Nigeria's first republic contributed significantly to north-south polarization; the differently structured federalism of the second republic was not conducive to the same result. Malaysia's heterogeneous constituencies combined with some idiosyncratic circumstances to propel formation of a multiethnic coalition; Sri Lanka's homogeneous constituencies produced Sinhalese governments with no reason to include the Tamils. There are many institutions compatible with democracy in the abstract, but not all of them are conducive to multiethnic inclusiveness.

As a matter of fact, much of what passes for the usual democratic rules either does nothing about ethnic exclusion or actually fosters it. Those rules may work well enough where ethnic cleavages are not sharp, so political affiliations are fluid, and majorities and minorities can be made and unmade. The same rules work differently where divisions are seen to be ascriptive and therefore immutable and where, as is common in such societies, political parties are ethnically based. Consider five paradigmatic cases of the relations among voters, parties, and election results—all in the context of free and fair elections.

1) One set of voters, represented by one party, comprises a majority of votes, and its party wins a majority of seats in a parliamentary system. If the rules of contestation are working to keep open the possibility of alternation in office, the minority need only wait for another day to augment its ranks and reverse the result. But suppose the majority and minority are fixed rather than fluid, because each thinks of itself as a group defined by birth and possessing affinities and interests not shared across group lines. Two consequences follow. Parties that span group lines will be difficult to organize, and in the existing bifurcated situation alternation in office is highly improbable. The textbook case of democratic majority rule turns quickly into a case of egregious minority exclusion. In ethnically divided societies, majority rule is not a solution; it is a problem, because it permits domination, apparently in perpetuity.

2) Examine next a more subtle, equally disturbing version of the same problem. Suppose there are three parties, two with 40-percent support each and one with 20 percent. Divided over strategy, the 20-percent party splits, the slightly larger segment lining up with one of the 40-percent parties to form a government. Predictable power relations put the smaller partner in a distinctly inferior position, such that the larger party nearly rules alone. Now a minority rules the rest, but in a situation of such instability that new elections can produce a different configuration—unless, of course, these parties represent ethnic groups whose members will generally not support parties across group lines. In that case, minority rule may prove durable.

3) So far I have ignored any disparity between votes cast and seats won. Problems 1 and 2 would be unaffected by proportional representation: it has been postulated that the seats won are proportionate to party strength. But suppose an Anglo-American plurality electoral system, in which a seat is won by whichever candidate receives the largest number of votes, even if less than 50 percent. Parties can easily put together majorities under such a system with less than half of the total vote. Margaret Thatcher's Tories, thrice elected with significant parliamentary majorities, never received more than 44 percent of the vote. We might think of fairer ways to conduct British elections, but no one thinks the possibility of democratic alternation in office is shut off under this system. If Britain were an ethnically divided society, however, and the Conservatives, Labourites, and Liberal Democrats each represented a single ethnic group, the claim of permanent tyranny of a minority would be extremely plausible.

Now if the first case involved a too-faithful reflection of ethnic divisions, resulting in the inclusion of the majority and the exclusion of the minority, the two cases of minority rule result from distortions due, respectively, to the distribution of cleavages within the 20-percent group and to the way the electoral system converts votes to seats. And if the electoral system distortion were removed—for example, by proportional representation—problem 3 would simply become a variant of problem 2. It would, however, still be a problem.

There are two other sources of distortion that can produce minority rule as a result of procedurally free and fair elections. One possible source is federalism; another derives from the dynamics of coalitions.

4) Suppose, in a federal system, there are three states or provinces, one significantly larger than the other two, so that its population is equal to that of those two combined. The largest group in the largest state has two-thirds of the voting population in that state, but one-third in the country as a whole. There is no significant devolution of power below the state level. Since the largest group in the largest state dominates politics in that state, the growth of minority-based opposition parties is inhibited there, for they could never hope to control the state. In national elections, the votes of that large state are sufficient to provide fully 50 percent of the parliamentary seats for its regionally based party, which then has every prospect of forming a government. In this way, a regional majority—but a minority nationally—has used its control of its home state as a vehicle for minority rule. It has, in a sense, received a seat bonus from federalism comparable to the one that plurality elections often provide the largest party.

5) Coalition politics can also produce minority rule. Assume that several ethnic groups all divide their votes between two or more parties, each of them representing only that group. One of the groups, however, is larger than the others; it comprises about half the total population, and it divides its vote between two parties in a ratio of two-to-one. Other groups divide their vote among several parties more or less evenly. The largest party thus receives two-thirds of the votes of the largest group, totaling about one-third of all votes cast. That party becomes the core of a governing coalition that includes at least one party from each of the other groups. All other parties are left in opposition. By dominating the coalition, the core party can essentially rule the country with the support of two-thirds of its group, one-third of the voting population. In a plurality electoral system, it will win more than one-third of the total seats on its one-third of the vote, but that merely enhances its already favorable position. None of this would ordinarily raise any eyebrows, except that this party is ethnically based, and the policy output of the coalition is thus skewed in favor of its group.

As a matter of fact, none of these possibilities is hypothetical; each depicts politics in some multiethnic society.[8] In each, the democratic problem results from the fixity of party boundaries, which end at group boundaries, even though some groups are represented by more than one party. To be sure, some of the exclusions produced by these configurations are more egregious than others. If majorities shut out minorities clearly and permanently, as they did repeatedly in Sri Lanka, it is not surprising that the sense of exclusion might ultimately produce large-scale violence. If minorities or pluralities shut out majorities, or even if they shut out pluralities or other minorities, as they did in Nigeria because of its asymmetric federalism, the result is also likely to be instability. If, however, minorities or pluralities manage to coopt fractions of several other groups in a coalition, as the leading Malay party has in Malaysia,[9] the result may not quite be seen as complete exclusion, but as a galling, frustrating partial exclusion—not a *casus belli*, but not an arrangement that generates intense loyalty to the system either.

In every one of these illustrations, the results could be brought about under conditions perfectly consistent with the procedural assumptions of democracy. The results are an artifact of the interaction of demography with the rules of the game. Purely procedural conceptions of democracy are thus inadequate for ethnically divided polities, for the procedure can be impeccable and the exclusion complete.

There are possibilities for changing the rules of the game to make them function better in such societies—and to foster inclusiveness—though this is never easy. Whether we mean by democracy the realistic possibility of contest and alternation or participation that is more inclusive than the mere prospect of alternation implies, this much is clear: the fixed character of allegiances is what permits majorities to exclude minorities and minorities to exclude majorities. There are, then, only two problems of democracy in severely divided societies: majority rule and minority rule. Those two problems, however, cover a great deal of territory.

Democratic Remediation

In the face of this rather dismal account, first of the concrete failures of democracy in divided societies and then of the inadequacy of most decision rules and institutions to deal with the conditions underlying these failures of inclusion, one is tempted to throw up one's hands. What is the point of holding elections if all they do in the end is to substitute a Bemba-dominated regime for a Nyanja regime in Zambia, the two equally narrow, or a southern regime for a northern one in Benin, neither incorporating the other half of the state?

For some, the answer to this dilemma is to remove ethnicity from politics. The assumption is that class or ideology is a more genuine basis of political alignment or that ethnicity is, for all purposes, poisonous to political health. A recent example of this tendency is the decision of the Nigerian military authorities to permit only two parties, one social democratic and one conservative, both by fiat multiethnic. The artificiality of this solution, its premise that ethnicity performs no legitimate political functions, and the unlikelihood that such powerful affiliations can simply be written out of the political process all stamp it as unwise. Ethnic affiliations provide a sense of security in a divided society, as well as a source of trust, certainty, reciprocal help, and protection against neglect of one's interests by strangers. In divided societies, the sense of an ethnic group as a community and its competition with others to constitute the whole community create a strong impetus toward party organization along ethnic lines.

> "Ethnic affiliations provide a sense of security in a divided society, as well as a source of trust, certainty, reciprocal help, and protection against neglect of one's interests by strangers."

For others, the answer is to develop norms of ethnic inclusiveness, manifested in a single, grand coalition following rules of proportional distribution and allowing group vetoes of collective decisions. Among the many defects of this solution, there is one that it shares with the abolition-of-ethnicity solution: *ex cathedra*, it simply advises participants in ethnic conflict to put their conflict aside. Why a party that thinks it can win might do this for the benefit of its opponents is, at the least, mysterious. Moreover, the wholly inclusive grand coalition runs squarely into the problem of distribution. If, under these decision rules, everyone is included, if distributive shares are fixed, and if minorities that would be voiceless if left in opposition are accorded not merely a voice but a veto, what is the reward of winning? As we have seen, the election of a too-inclusive multiethnic government (as in Zambia) merely marks the commencement of a new struggle for inclusion and exclusion. The recurrent character of that struggle suggests that these decision rules will not be adopted and, more importantly, will not survive if adopted. It is one thing to demand acknowledgment that those left in opposition are merely outside the government but not outside the community; it is quite another to require that no one be left outside the government.

Since multiethnic parties like the Zambian MMD tend to decompose in severely divided societies, interethnic coalitions have much to commend them. But even if they can be formed, coalitions that include everyone are unlikely to be durable in divided societies. Two other types are possible, and it is worth thinking about how they can be fostered. Significantly, both do their compromising before elections.

The first, exemplified by Malaysia, is the multiethnic coalition flanked by ethnic parties that oppose the coalition's compromises. Some members of all groups are in the coalition, but it is not a grand coalition. The coalition was formed before independence, in the 1950s, at a time when the roughly 50-50 division between Malays and non-Malays created electoral uncertainties. Without a coalition, it was doubtful that the leading Malay party could have won the forthcoming municipal elections, in which Chinese votes would be crucial, and, after Chinese were granted citizenship, the postindependence parliamentary elections as well. In other words, electoral incentives were at the root of the coalition. The coalition then assumed a permanent form and ran candidates on a single slate, so that they could benefit from the pooling of Malay and non-Malay votes in any constituency. The only way to pool votes across ethnic lines was to present a moderate face to the electorate, so voters of one group could be induced to vote for candidates of another. Hence the coalition was dependent on compromise.

From the very beginning, Malay parties on the flank objected to compromises with the Chinese, whose citizenship they thought illegitimate. Non-Malay parties on the other flank objected to anything other than full equality for all citizens. Inside the coalition, the strong Malay claim to indigenousness and the larger number of Malay voters supporting the coalition weighted outputs toward the Malay side, particularly after 1970. Indeed, the rules of the game itself—such as constituency delimitation—were also subject to the greater power of the Malay partner, so that the power of the non-Malays in the coalition eroded. Nevertheless, the coalition was and is at least a guarantee against total exclusion.

The coalition system in the Indian state of Kerala also emerged in idiosyncratic circumstances, and it has suffered less slippage and ethnic skewing over time. Kerala has four main politically influential groups: Christians, Nairs (high-caste Hindus), Ezhava (low-caste Hindus), and Muslims. In the 1950s and 1960s, it became clear that no one or two groups could rule the state alone. Eventually, the state settled into a system of competing coalitions, each more or less inclusive of some members of all the major groups, though in varying proportions over time. Although all groups sooner or later exercise some power, this is not a grand coalition; there is always a powerful opposition. A group or a leader of a fraction of a group, discontented with what is offered by one coalition, can offer its support to the alternative coalition, which might weight group interests differently. In constituencies with varying degrees of heterogeneity, votes are pooled across ethnic lines to support coalition candidates.

The program of each coalition is necessarily a compromise whose exact shape depends on the relative weight of its participants. But in this deeply divided society, exclusion is most unlikely to be permanent:

the coalitions are fluid. Moreover, the existence of competing coalitions encourages splits within ethnic groups, so that one fraction might align with one coalition, another fraction with the other. Fluidity begets fluidity. In a country increasingly beset with every form of ethnic violence, Kerala is a conspicuous exception.[10]

The exceptional character of Kerala is not due to an absence of conflict or bitterly contested issues. Quite the contrary: the disadvantaged Ezhava community has longstanding grievances against the Nairs; Hindus and Muslims fear each other; and both fear the power of the Christians, who in turn suspect the Nairs of harboring intentions to dominate. Kerala's coalitions do not follow from moderate conflict; instead, the coalitions moderate the conflict.

Four conditions underpinned the growth of Kerala's competing coalitions. First, the state's multipolar fluidity made it clear that some form of coalition was inevitable. Second, the coalitions made (and make) preelection agreements and, since they each ran a single slate, allocated seats centrally. Consequently, as in Malaysia, voters in one group had to be induced to vote for candidates of another—which can only happen if there is compromise on ethnic issues. Third, whereas Malay claims to priority left only opportunities on the ethnic flanks and divided the party spectrum into three parts—Malay, interethnic, and non-Malay—no group in Kerala could claim to be more indigenous than any other. As a result, disappointed claimants could turn to a competing coalition rather than being relegated to root-and-branch opposition to compromise *per se*. This rendered the system less liable to dangerous swings of ethnic discontent. A change of government simply brings a different multiethnic coalition to power. Fourth, the coalitions were, in the first instance, centered around national-level Indian parties that were ostensibly nonethnic: Congress and the Communists. Ethnic groups kept their own state-level parties, but some leaders also entered these national parties. Had Kerala not initially possessed these nonethnic vehicles for ethnic aspirations to begin the process of compromise and coalition, one wonders whether the state's politics would have developed in the benign way it has.

Building Accommodative Institutions

Idiosyncrasy, then, played a major role in the formation of both the Malaysia and Kerala coalitions. It is not surprising that few other accommodative institutions of these kinds can be found in severely divided societies. It is not that we are wholly ignorant about how to structure electoral systems to build in incentives for interethnic accommodation or how to create federal states so as to reduce bifurcation and enhance multipolar fluidity. Ethnic alignments are sensitive to political context; if multipolar fluidity is present, means can

probably be found to preserve it. Politicians are notably responsive to
political incentives, and if preelection vote-pooling coalitions are what
divided societies need, means can be found to those ends, too, in at
least some conflict-prone polities. But little effective planning has been
done to promote accommodative institutions. Virtually by accident,
Malaysia and Kerala show that where ethnic parties have strong political
incentives to compromise, they will do so. Elsewhere, the few efforts
at promoting interethnic accommodation in a concerted way have largely
taken the form of constitutional prescriptions, *dehors* the political
incentive structure, for a minority veto, or disproportionate minority
influence in government, or a separation of powers, or parties that are
forbidden to make ethnic appeals. The shallow foundations of most of
these proposals—their insufficient grounding either in the ongoing
interests of politicians or in a careful diagnosis of what was likely to
go wrong—virtually assured their failure.

Constitution makers in new democracies have often been content to
restore the very institutions that were conducive to the previous ethnic
breakdown, or else to look for inspiration to the institutions of either
the former colonialists or more broadly to the apparently successful
major democracies of the West. Unsurprisingly, Francophone states tend
to have borrowed French institutions; Anglophone states tend to have
borrowed British institutions. And more than a few provision merchants
from the United States have sold ready-made constitutional clauses to
Africans, Asians, and East Europeans eager for their talismanic value,
even though they had been fashioned for the conditions of American
democracy rather than their own. As the recent wave of
democratizations now runs its course, it is not too soon to say that a
major opportunity for constitutional planning for interethnic
accommodation has largely been lost, and the emerging results are there
for all to see. This is a serious foreign-policy failure for the United
States and for the Western world more generally.

That is not to say that the exercise would have been easy. If the key
is to secure the adoption of electoral and governmental structures that
give politicians incentives to behave in one way rather than
another—and this *is* the key—there are still many obstacles to achieving
this result. Most of the time, political leaders sense some advantage in
pursuing conflict rather than accommodation and so would be loath to
accept institutions that structure incentives differently. Furthermore,
spotty innovations that create a few incentives in one direction are often
overcome by other innovations that create countervailing incentives.

A coherent package, even a redundant package, of conflict-reducing
techniques is required.[11] Such a package would include electoral systems
to create ongoing incentives for interethnic cooperation and for
preelection coalitions based on vote pooling. For many countries, there
would also be provisions for federalism or regional autonomy.

Combined with policies that give regionally concentrated groups a strong stake in the center, devolution can help avert separatism. The skillful division of territory can foster multipolar fluidity where it exists and prevent bifurcation; it can also produce commonalities among similarly situated regional units that cross ethnic lines; and it can give politicians a chance to practice conciliation before they arrive at the center.

> *"Conciliatory rules put in the form of constraints have often been neglected or overthrown by politicians who found nothing in their self-interest to support them."*

All such innovations are difficult to introduce with sufficient coherence to have their intended effect. There are alternative ways to view electoral systems that give priority to goals such as proportionality of seats to votes, or the accountability of representatives, or the mandate and durability of governments—all otherwise worthy goals that, in a severely divided society, ought to be subordinated to the lifesaving goal of making interethnic moderation rewarding. There is the risk that planners may neglect the ongoing incentives facing the politicians who will have to operate the system, and may instead adopt requirements of behavior that are just in the abstract but not firmly anchored in those incentives. Conciliatory rules put in the form of constraints have often been neglected or overthrown by politicians who found nothing in their self-interest to support them. Moreover, a coherent package would have to be approved in a forum to which contestants come to negotiate a compromise. Compromise has many virtues, but consistency of purpose and coherence of outcome are not usually among them. There will therefore generally be some disjunction between what needs to be adopted and the process by which it will be adopted.

There are moments when political leaders see or can be induced to see the advantages of accommodation. One such moment occurred in Nigeria in 1978, when civilian leaders were pondering what institutions should supplant the receding military regime. Chastened by a destructive civil war, they did not know who would be hurt next time if the same conditions recurred, and they behaved as if they wore John Rawls's veil of ignorance. This posture was conducive to some sensible innovations (although some of them were later swamped by institutions with countervailing incentives). In at least some countries redemocratizing after bitter experiences of Soviet or African or Asian single-party or military rule, some leaders might have been induced to adopt a similar posture, and a more careful focus on diagnosis and prescription might have emerged. For most, that moment has passed. As things stand, many countries seem headed for a rerun of their earlier experience.

When Nigeria returned to civilian rule in 1979, it soon became clear that more obstacles were arrayed against the project than had been arrayed against the democracy that was launched at independence. A bloated, greedy military had emerged out of the earlier ethnic conflicts, civil war, and authoritarian rule. It would have been highly advantageous to have set democratic, conciliatory institutions firmly on course the first time. The same will generally be true elsewhere. To have failed once makes things more difficult the next time. To have failed twice makes the next time problematic altogether. Many states will soon be in this position. In planning for a state that is to be democratic and multiethnic, earlier is assuredly better.

NOTES

The author gratefully acknowledges research assistance provided by Natalie Kay Sidles.

1. See René Lemarchand, "African Transitions to Democracy: An Interim (and Mostly Pessimistic) Assessment," *Africa Insight* 22 (1992): 178-85.

2. Cameron McWhirter and Gur Melamede, "Ethiopia: The Ethnicity Factor," *Africa Report*, September-October 1992, 30-33.

3. Daria Fane, "Moldova: Breaking Loose from Moscow," in Ian Bremmer and Ray Taras, eds., *Nations and Politics in the Soviet Successor States*, (Cambridge: Cambridge University Press, 1993), 121-53; Vladimir Socor, "Moldova's 'Dniester' Ulcer," *RFE/RL Research Report*, January 1993, 12-16.

4. Stephen Jones, "Georgia: A Failed Democratic Transition," in Bremmer and Taras, op. cit., 288-310.

5. See, e.g., Marinus H. van Ijzendoorn, "Moral Judgment, Authoritarianism, and Ethnocentrism," *Journal of Social Psychology* 129 (1989): 37-45.

6. The relations between ethnic conflict and single-party regimes are traced in Donald L. Horowitz, *Ethnic Groups in Conflict* (Berkeley: University of California Press, 1985), 429-37.

7. For the results by province, see *The October 31, 1991, National Elections in Zambia* (Washington, D.C.: National Democratic Institute for International Affairs and Carter Center of Emory University, 1992), 165.

8. The first case exemplifies Sri Lanka, Sudan, and many other countries where minorities have experienced fairly straightforward exclusion. The second, with variable percentages, depicts roughly what happened after independence in the initially tripolar conflicts of Nigeria and Congo (Brazzaville). Absent unusual institutional arrangements, tripolar contests have tended to become bipolar, as the weakest party chooses to align with one of the other contestants or as the least cohesive splits and divides its support. In parliamentary systems, this is attributable to the strong pressure to attain a majority of seats, which is converted into pressure on a small or less cohesive third group by larger actors. The third case is typical of countries where a cohesive plurality confronts smaller or less cohesive groups in a first-past-the-post electoral system, such as the one Guyana had before the British changed it in the 1960s and the one Kenya now has. Before the change in Guyana, an East Indian-dominated party gained 57 percent of the seats on less than 43 percent of the vote. In the 1992 Kenyan elections, Moi's ethnically limited party won 53 percent of the seats on a mere 31 percent of the vote. The fourth case recapitulates the asymmetric federalism of Nigeria's First Republic (1960-66), which was responsible for the inflated representation of a Hausa-Fulani-dominated party in national politics. When the Northern Region was later broken up into 10 states, it could no longer

be used to provide the equivalent of a seat bonus. Hausa-Fulani power in the First Republic was thus magnified by a combination of the conditions described in the second and fourth examples. The fifth case is a reasonably faithful description of the circumstances that have sustained the dominant position of the United Malays National Organization (UMNO) in the Malaysian coalition, although UMNO receives not more than one-third of the total vote. See note 9 below.

9. In the Malaysian case, the result is facilitated by distortions resulting from constituency malapportionment favoring Malays, as well as the seat bonus from first-past-the-post, so that one-third of the vote or less recurrently secures for the dominant party in the coalition (the United Malays National Organization) between 40 and 50 percent of the seats. (In making these calculations, I have excluded the numerous vote transfers among the coalition partners, which result from the fact that the coalition runs on a single slate.) See *Malaysian General Election, 1990: An Analysis Presented at a Forum Held on October 25, 1990 at Maktab Kerjasama* (Kuala Lumpur: I & J Sdn. Bhd., 1990; computer printout); *Elections in Malaysia: A Handbook of Facts and Figures on the Elections, 1955-1986* (Kuala Lumpur: NSTP Research and Information Services, 1990).

10. See E.J. Thomas, *Coalition Game Politics in Kerala* (New Delhi: Intellectual Publishing House, 1985); N. Jose Chander, ed., *Dynamics of State Politics: Kerala* (New Delhi: Sterling Publishers Private, 1986).

11. I have discussed such techniques in *Ethnic Groups in Conflict*, 563-652, and *A Democratic South Africa? Constitutional Engineering in a Divided Society* (Berkeley: University of California Press, 1991), 124-226.

4.
THE TRAVAILS OF FEDERALISM IN NIGERIA

Rotimi T. Suberu

Rotimi T. Suberu is lecturer in political science at the University of Ibadan, Nigeria, and a 1993-94 Peace Fellow at the United States Institute of Peace in Washington, D.C. He has published several articles on the Nigerian federal system and is currently preparing a book-length study of federalism, democracy, and ethnic-conflict management in Nigeria.

The need to establish a stable system of federal democracy has dominated the history of constitutional discourse and design in Nigeria since the winning of independence from Britain and the inauguration of the First Republic in 1960. Throughout the period of military government that began in 1966 and ended with the establishment of the Second Republic (1979-83), and right on up to current efforts to reintroduce civilian rule, Nigeria has searched for a federal arrangement that can accommodate its combustible ethnic, regional, and religious divisions. This search has been complicated by the instability and vulnerability of competitive civilian politics, the political hegemony of centralizing military elites, the perverse distributive pressures inherent in the country's oil-based economy, and growing disagreement among key elites regarding the design of key federal institutions.

Nigeria's several hundred ethnolinguistic groups were formally consolidated into a single country in 1914 following a protracted and uneven process of British colonial conquest and incorporation. The largest of these groups are the Muslim Hausa-Fulani, the predominantly Christian Igbo, and the religiously bicommunal Yoruba; together they comprise approximately two-thirds of Nigeria's estimated population of 88.5 million. The rest of this population is made up of more than two hundred "ethnic minorities," ranging in size from several thousand to a few million and comprising adherents of Christianity, Islam, and traditional indigenous religions.

Although these diverse peoples had been interacting with one another in various ways since long before the colonial era, the sheer artificiality of the British-drawn boundaries, the relatively centralized ethnic structure (with just three groups predominating), and the uneven modernization and differential administration of the country under colonial rule engendered strong regionalist pressures for the replacement of the unitary (albeit decentralized) colonial administration with full-fledged federalism. This transition finally occurred in 1954 with the inauguration of a triregional federal framework, which secured autonomy and hegemony for the Hausa-Fulani, Yoruba, and Igbo nationalities in the Northern, Western, and Eastern regions respectively.

The problem with this federal structure lay not only in its inequitable incorporation of minority communities into a set of regional bastions dominated by large ethnic groups, but also in the overwhelming size of the Northern region, which included nearly three-quarters of the country's territory and over half of its population. The creation of the Midwest region in 1963, while giving satisfaction to ethnic-minority aspirations in the old Western region, left the country's minority problem substantially unresolved and intensified the overall imbalance in the structure of the Federation.

Nigeria: Ethnic Groups and Four Regions
From Crawford Young, *The Politics of Cultural Pluralism*
(Madison: University of Wisconsin Press, 1976). Reprinted with permission.

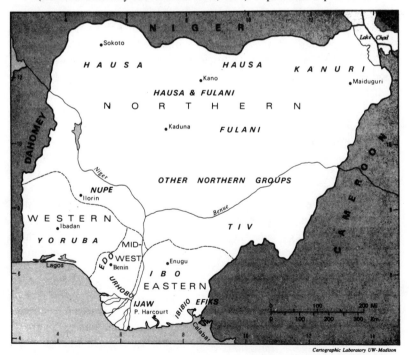

This imbalance played a large role in bringing about the collapse of the First Republic and the imposition of military rule in January 1966. Also contributing to that turn of events were the ethnoregional polarization of party competition, the increasingly vicious struggle for political advantage among regions, and, in particular, the politically motivated sacking of the Western regional government by the federal administration in 1962 and its turbulent aftermath.

Although bedeviled by severe tensions that culminated in the horrific Biafran civil war of 1967-70, the period of military rule that followed the collapse of the First Republic did succeed in transforming the country into a federation of 12 (later 19) states. This multistate federalism in turn helped to secure support for a united Nigeria from ethnic-minority communities in the secessionist Eastern region, to dilute the hegemony of the north, to distribute elements of the larger ethnic groups across more states, to furnish local administrative outlets for the huge oil windfalls of the 1970s, and, in general, to contain the disintegrative tendencies inherent in Nigeria's cultural diversity.

In designing the Second Republic, military leaders and their civilian advisors predictably sought to reinforce the integrative effects of the multistate structure. This was to be accomplished via the promulgation of a highly centralized federal constitution. Among other things, the new constitution would establish a uniform system of local government, replace the First Republic's Westminster parliamentary system with an American-style presidential model, and require that the plural nature or "federal character" of the country be reflected in the election of the president, the formation of political parties, and the composition and conduct of public agencies.

It is generally conceded that these structural and institutional changes helped to ensure "that the kind of ethnic and regional polarization that savaged the First Republic did not emerge in the Second Republic."[1] Nevertheless, the "boomerang effects" of some of these changes were apparent in the abuses and controversies that beset attempts to apply the "federal character" principle at the national level; in the vociferous campaigns for creating new states by communities thirsting for access to federal revenues; and in the virulent antagonism that state governments dominated by opposition parties showed toward the centralizing features of the 1979 Constitution. Some of these governments were eventually uprooted in the rigged 1983 elections, which established the hegemony of the ruling National Party of Nigeria (NPN) and precipitated a military coup at the end of that year. Thus in both the First and Second Republics, the ruling elite at the center betrayed its weak commitment to federalism and toleration by crudely attempting to dislodge its opponents in the states.

Since the military reimposed itself as the ruler of Nigeria in 1983, there has been a sweeping centralization of the federal system and an intensification of ethnic, regional, and religious tensions. The presidency of General Ibrahim Babangida, who ousted General Muhammad Buhari in August 1985, has seen the states considerably weakened via fragmentation into smaller units (now 30 in number), cuts in their shares of federal revenues, and systematic erosion of the powers that they had once wielded over local authorities. The Babangida regime's centralizing impulses have received powerful reinforcement from a system in which federal petroleum taxes and mining rents and royalties comprise more than four-fifths of all public revenues at every level of government. This arrangement has a double effect, providing a strong inducement to communal demands for new—and, of course, federally funded—governmental units even as it unleashes "strong pressures towards financial unification and the end of federalism."[2]

In the political sphere, Babangida's major centralizing initiative has been to restrict civilian political competition to two parties that his government imposed: the National Republican Convention (NRC) and the Social Democratic Party (SDP). This mandatory two-party system provided the basis for elections to local councils, state governorships and legislatures, and the National Assembly during December 1990, December 1991, and July 1992, respectively. Its fragility was exposed in June 1993, however, when the Babangida government cancelled the presidential election, won by a southerner (the SDP's candidate Moshood Abiola) for the first time ever in the country's history

At the same time, there has been an upsurge of tension over the "national question" and the worth of the institutions that the Third Republic has put in place to stave off destructive divisiveness. In April 1990, the nation was momentarily confronted with the specter of another civil war when disgruntled military officers sought unsuccessfully to remove Babangida from power and to "excise" the five Muslim states of the far north from the federation.

Religious Turbulence

Smoldering ethnic, regional, or religious tensions in Africa have often been fanned into full-blown conflict by the arbitrary, drastic, and heavyhanded actions of unelected authoritarian regimes. Apart from General Johnson Aguiyi-Ironsi's disastrous attempts to impose a unitary system on Nigeria in May 1966, probably no single action of a Nigerian government has stirred the waters of sectional conflict as vigorously as the Babangida government's surprise move enrolling the country in the 45-member Organization of the Islamic Conference (OIC) in January 1986. Since the OIC controversy, Christian-Muslim antipathies in Nigeria have crystallized ominously around such issues as the definition of the secularity of the Nigerian state, the constitutional status of *shari'a,* the religious affiliations of officeholders in key public institutions, the appropriate role for the government in the organization of religious pilgrimages, the allocation of air time to religious programming on public media, and the construction of places of worship in government buildings. Other incendiary religious issues have included the allocation of public land to religious bodies, the teaching of religious subjects in educational institutions, governmental policies toward Israel and the Middle East, and most importantly, the trial and conviction by federally appointed judicial panels of Muslim youths and Christian ethnic-minority elites implicated in some of the religious disturbances that have convulsed northern Nigeria since 1987.

Indeed, recent religious mobilization in Nigeria has fueled the longstanding grievances of non-Muslims living within the mostly Muslim north. Thousands of lives have been lost since the late 1980s in the states of Kaduna and Bauchi as non-Muslim minority communities staged bloody uprisings to protest their cultural and economic subordination under the Fulani emirate system and the power of Hausa settlers. These communal disturbances invariably spilled over into major northern cities like Bauchi, Kaduna, and Zaria, where vengeful Muslim mobs visited mayhem, death, and destruction on non-Muslim communities, including southern migrant groups. Ethnoreligious violence also claimed up to a hundred lives in Kano and Taraba states during October 1991 and March 1992. Finally, in January 1993, a faction of the millenarian Maitatsine movement (a heretical offshoot of Islam), notorious for its bloody confrontations with state security forces throughout the early 1980s, unleashed mayhem in Funtua, Katsina, killing at least 34 persons and exploding all the military's claims about the suppression of this group.

This religious turbulence has resonated sharply in the regional struggles for power in Nigeria. Thus the Christian Association of Nigeria (CAN) has been in the forefront of those complaining about northern-Muslim predominance in Babangida's administration, while the Roman Catholic Archdiocese of Lagos has sought openly to identify with demands that the first president of the Third Republic be a southerner. When northern-Muslim presidential aspirants triumphed decisively over southerners in the two parties' brazenly manipulated (and eventually nullified) primaries of August and September 1992, CAN leader Benson Idahosa threatened a Christian boycott of the presidential election and "a situation that is worse than civil war."[3] After a northern Muslim and a southern (Yoruba) Muslim were nominated to be the presidential standardbearers of the NRC and the SDP, respectively, debate came to focus on whether the vice-presidential candidates of both parties had to be Christians, as demanded by many Christian elements. In the end, the NRC chose an Igbo Christian and the SDP a northern non-Hausa Muslim, giving the latter a regionally but not religiously balanced ticket. Nevertheless, that ticket appears to have won a resounding victory of unprecedently clear and national proportions, with support from every major section of the country.

Such religious contention is particularly sharp because the two previous Nigerian Republics were led by northern Muslims, while northerners generally have headed the federal government for 29 of the 33 years since independence. This has engendered southern demands for the rotation of the presidency on a regional basis not only as a means of ensuring a more equitable sharing of federal power, but also as a legitimate complement to the continuing use of quotas and the "federal character" principle to reduce southern domination of educational and bureaucratic institutions. Such an alternation scheme is predictably unpopular in the north, where it is often denounced as antidemocratic and intended to deprive the region of its only cushion against southern, specifically Yoruba, socioeconomic preeminence. This is a major reason why Babangida's cancellation of the June 1993 presidential election, before the results were completely announced but after it was apparent that Abiola had clearly won, provoked a crisis not merely for democracy, but for the future of regional and ethnic relations in the country. More than any previous elections, the June contest has emerged as a test of whether a southerner will ever be permitted to win power at the center.

Regional Rivalries

Regional rivalries have been a primary source of the political explosiveness of population counts in Nigeria. The 1991 census, owing largely to its astute design and execution (religious and ethnic questions were excluded, for instance) and to its relative comparability with the preindependence 1952-53 count, had fewer polarizing effects than did the postindependence censuses of 1962-63 and 1973. The provisional 1991 results, however, indicate a continuing northern demographic majority of 53 percent. Recent statements by leading southern politicians and newspapers suggest that southern opinion continues to regard this northern majority as both a political nightmare and a demographic threat.

The new census figures have provoked trenchant criticism and charges of undercounting from most state governments, local authorities, and communities. In fact, by some demographic projections, the total count may understate Nigeria's population by as much as 10 million or more. Additionally, the census has generated considerable ethnic controversy in states like Kogi and Ondo, where the new figures contradict the assumed demographic balance between blocs of the population.

In all, the tribunals that have been set up to investigate and resolve complaints arising from the 1991 census will have to contend with a

total of 131 petitions involving 27 of the 30 states. The volume of
litigation is not surprising given the major role that population statistics
play in the allocation of revenues and political representation, the
creation of new political units, and the citing of infrastructure
improvements.

Partly in order to defuse the census issue, however, current revenue-
sharing arrangements allot 40 percent of federal disbursements to states
and localities on the basis of "inter-unit equality," with only 30 percent
(instead of the previous 40-to-50 percent) allotted on the basis of
population figures. Despite the existence of divergent interests among
the states, and the incentive that the standard of "inter-unit equality"
gives to communal pressures for the creation of new states and
localities, this formula has proven less contentious than its predecessor.

Other changes incorporated in the new revenue-sharing formula
reflect the military government's commitment to the constitutional,
functional, and financial empowerment of the local governments, each
of which is now equipped with the full apparatus of a presidential-style
executive branch. The share of federally collected revenues assigned to
local governments is now 20 percent (up from 10 percent during the
Second Republic), while the share assigned to the states has declined
from 30.5 to 24 percent. The relative decline in the share of federal
revenue going to the states, coming at a time when their number has
gone from 19 to 30, has angered all the state governments and roused
fears about the imminent collapse of Nigerian federalism.

The most intense opponents of current revenue-sharing policies are
the communities of ethnic-minority groups who live in or near the oil-
rich Niger Delta. These southerners have used means ranging from
peaceful demonstrations to willful sabotage of oil explorations and
violent agitations to press their fiscal and ecological concerns. In
particular, these communities want a further increase in federal grants
to the oil-producing areas (the allocation went up in June 1992 from 1.5
to 3 percent of mineral revenues), as well as more say in the doings
of the new presidentially appointed Oil Mineral Producing Areas
Development Commission (OMPADEC). At its most extreme, this
ethnic-minority opposition backs a shift to loose confederalism as the
only alternative to the expropriation of Delta resources "for the
exclusive benefit of the majority groups."[4]

The conflict over oil revenues has also been fueled by Babangida's
lavish creation of new states and localities. Apart from increasing the
number of states (to 21 in 1987 and then to 30 in 1991), Babangida
has also expanded the number of local government areas from 301 in
1984 to 449 in 1989 and to 589 in 1991. There are strong indications
that the number will be increased to at least 600 before the military
finally disengages from power. In the wake of these reorganizations,
five things have become apparent. First, ethnic minorities increasingly

oppose what they regard as the rigging of the state structure to secure more federal funds for the large nationalities at the expense of minorities living in several of the ethnically heterogeneous states. Minority-group representatives condemn a situation in which the three big ethnic groups dominate 18 of the 30 states, while smaller peoples, including most of the oil-producing communities, "have been corralled into unitary . . . multiethnic states."[5]

Second, it is now obvious that political decentralization and financial redistribution can only be impeded, rather than promoted, by the strategy of dicing the country up into smaller and increasingly unviable states and localities, with the proliferation of inefficient state and local bureaucracies that comes along with it. Moreover, the proliferation of states is threatening to make a mockery of the "federal character" standard for national ministerial appointments, since with so many new states it becomes cumbersome or impossible to insist on the representation of every state.

Third, with the continuing implementation by state governments of educational and employment policies that discriminate against "nonindigenes," the proliferation of new states is a recipe for more state-based discrimination. As former head of state General Yakubu Gowon recently observed, "The creation of more states, instead of ensuring the unity of the Federation, could erode it."[6]

Fourth, it is apparent that the territorial fragmentation of each of the three major ethnic groups has not made them less cohesive at the national level. Indeed, despite the development of bitter, and sometimes bizarre, intraethnic conflicts within and among major-group states over local and regional issues, each of the three major groups continues to demonstrate remarkable solidarity as it competes with the others in bidding for supremacy in national politics. In essence, "the creation of states and the development of 'statism' have added—and not substituted—new patterns of cleavages to the preexisting ones."[7]

Fifth and finally, these reorganizations have not resolved or even eased the pressures for new constituent units, but have only succeeded in producing new ethnic or subethnic minorities, fresh political animosities, and renewed distributive pressures, leading to still more agitation for additional states or local government areas. There are fears that unless a way can be found to cap the process, the creation of new states and localities will become an "endless joke which will continue to reduce the viability of our federalism."[8]

Constitutional and Electoral Innovations

Nigeria's innovative, three-tiered federal constitution, with its provisions for federal, state, and local levels, remains key to promoting national integration and protecting vital segmental interests. The exclusive legislative powers of the federal government under the 1989 Constitution span the gamut from aviation, banking, elections, and mines and minerals through police, prisons, mail, and telegraphs to the promotion of an omnibus set of directive principles and objectives for public policy. The concurrent powers of the federal government and the states consist of some 12 items, including industrial, commercial, and agricultural development and postprimary education. Unenumerated residual powers generally belong to the states, but responsibility for primary education has been statutorily delegated to the reinvigorated local governments, which are also constitutionally required to participate in the socioeconomic programs of their state governments, and to undertake a number of independent functions of their own, including the gathering of vital statistics, the collection of taxes, and the provision of public conveniences.

This constitutional division of powers enables the states and localities to assume primary responsibility for many of the most important social services and programs. Even the modest decentralization envisioned by the Constitution, however, is undermined by the virtually complete dependence of the two lower tiers on federally collected oil revenues, and by the unwillingness of the federal government to accede to proposals for more extensive financial devolution to the constituent governments. Thus local governments have found themselves unable to run primary education successfully, and the states have recently had to rely on federal assistance to satisfy the wage demands of their employees, even as tight budgets have compelled both tiers to forgo any major new development expenditures.

Will the newly instituted mandatory two-party system bring about any change in the troubled dynamics of federalist politics in the Third Republic? In spite of its dubious legitimacy, the "two-party dictatorship"—to borrow a phrase from ex-governor Balarabe Musa—has effectively deflected the tendency for interparty competition in Nigeria to turn into a three-player game among the majority ethnic groups.[9] Although ethnic, regional, and religious influences are discernible in the patterns of local electoral support for the parties, the demonstrable success of each party in enlisting influential elites from *all* sections of the Federation has meant that interethnic competition has been rechanneled so that it is more intense within the parties than it is between them.

Like the NPN, which was the only party to achieve a truly national character in the Second Republic, both the NRC and the SDP have sought to sustain their ethnically variegated composition by resorting to "zoning" (i.e., the reservation of certain offices for specific regional or ethnic groups) and other informal extensions of federalism within the party system. In this regard, the two parties have not been deterred by the Federal Military Government's sanctimonious proscription of ethnoregional caucuses or groupings, within and outside the party system.

In March 1993, for instance, the SDP adopted an arrangement that "zoned" the party's presidential and vice-presidential candidates to the northeast and the Yoruba west or vice versa; the national chairmanship of the party and the deputy senate presidency to the southern minorities; the senate presidency and the post of party publicity secretary to the "Middle Belt" or the predominantly Christian lower north; the posts of speaker of the House of Representatives and party treasurer to the Igbo east; and the posts of deputy speaker of the House of Representatives and party secretary to the northwest. Additionally, a deputy chairman of the SDP is to be chosen from each of the party's six designated zones. Finally, if the "bloc-sharing formula" developed in 1991 by the Yoruba caucus of the SDP is approved, the most important ministries in an SDP federal cabinet will go to zones other than that of the incumbent president. This has the intended objective of taking some of the urgency out of the competition for the presidency.

The NRC, for its part, zoned its presidential nomination to the Muslim far north, the vice-presidential candidacy to the former Eastern region, the party chairmanship to the old Western region, and the post of party secretary to the Middle Belt.

These zoning schemes, which were not adopted in a manner free of intraparty controversy, have been developed as flexible rather than fixed arrangements, designed to achieve a broad representation of ethnoregional elites in key party positions while simultaneously rewarding the respective parties' strongest regional bases with the biggest plums, especially the presidential and vice-presidential nominations.

Sadly, the bold pragmatism that has characterized the conception and operation of the two-party system has been largely absent in the design of the electoral system. The single-member-constituency, first-past-the-post system has been retained from the First and Second Republics, despite well-articulated proposals for the introduction of some form of proportional representation. Among other consequences, this reliance on the old electoral system will sentence the Third Republic to the same problem that troubled the Second Republic—the tension between a legislature exclusively elected from narrow geographical constituencies and a nationally-based executive.

Two changes in electoral rules and arrangements must be noted, however. First, whereas a successful presidential candidate in the Second Republic was required to obtain a *plurality* of the total vote plus at least *one-quarter* of the votes cast in each of at least two-thirds of the Federation's states, such a candidate is now required, in view of the existence of only two parties, to obtain a *majority* of the total vote and at least *one-third* of the votes in two-thirds of the states. Failing this, the 1989 Constitution provides for a second election in which a successful candidate must obtain one-third of the votes in only a majority of the states or, in default of a conclusive second election, the selection of the president by a simple majority of votes cast in an electoral college comprising all members of the national and state legislatures. Comparable regulations guide the gubernatorial elections.

A second change in the electoral system has arisen from the federal government's August 1991 decision to establish local government areas, rather than population-based electoral districts, as the constituencies for the state legislatures and the federal House of Representatives. Under this scheme, which is aimed partly at depoliticizing the census, each local government area will produce two state legislators and one federal representative, while the federal senate has been retained as an upper house with three members from each state.[10]

Suffice it to say that this arrangement has engendered two controversial results. The first is the existence of imbalances in legislative representation grossly weighted against the more populous localities or states, especially Lagos. The other is the growing tendency toward instability and unwieldiness in a legislature that has become bloated because of persistent and politically irresistible communal pressures for the creation of new localities and the legislative seats they bring with them.

Proposals for Change

In Nigeria today, intense debate persists over the best way to provide for power sharing at the national level. This debate both has given rise to particular proposals that may help compensate for the limitations of the federal system and has generally illuminated the prospective course of constitutional discourse and development in Nigeria.

In 1988, for instance, a panel of the Constituent Assembly called for the creation of a three-person vice-presidency as a means of ensuring that more than just two ethnic groups could be represented at the apex of the federal executive. The full committee of the Assembly rejected this idea, however, partly on the grounds that it was weighted against minorities, partly because existing rules for the election of the president and vice president were considered sufficient to secure broad interethnic legitimacy, and partly because of concerns about shielding the panethnic ethos of the presidency from what many in the Assembly regarded as divisive ethnoregional claims. Nevertheless, variants of this proposal continue to enjoy the support of key opinion leaders, including Second Republic Vice President Alex Ekwueme.

A more modest, but more widely supported suggestion for modifying the present presidential system is the proposal for single, nonrenewable five- or six-year terms for the president and governors. This presumably would have the advantage of sharing power more widely over time while eliminating the abuses that always seem to accompany the reelection bids of Nigerian incumbents. Although the Political Bureau, the Constitutional Review Committee, and the Constituent Assembly made one of their rare shows of unanimity by endorsing this proposal, it was eventually quashed by the Babangida government, which decided to stay with the renewable four-year terms used in the Second Republic.

Equally strong support is developing among prominent Nigerians for the introduction of a French-style presidential-parliamentary model to help balance and expand the regional base of federal executive power. It has been suggested, for instance, that the combination of a popularly elected northern Muslim president and a southern Christian prime minister, or vice versa, would effectively defuse much of the regional polarization that continues to plague Nigerian politics. This, however, could lead to the kind of legitimacy crisis that beset the parliamentary First Republic when, in the aftermath of the disputed 1964 parliamentary election, there was a struggle for control between the northern Muslim prime minister and the southern Christian (largely ceremonial) president.

Although Babangida has repeatedly proclaimed the inviolability of the American-style presidential system in Nigeria, the interim administrative changes he announced in November 1992 amount to an implicit endorsement of the presidential-parliamentary model. While Babangida (a northern Muslim) kept his post as military president of the country, a Yoruba Christian was named as head of government and chairman of a 26-member Transitional (Ministerial) Council. The impact of the presidential-parliamentary model on future constitutional engineering in Nigeria may well depend on the perceived achievements or inadequacies of this interim experiment. Suffice it to say, however, that the experiment may have been tarnished by the growing suspicion that it is designed to perpetuate Babangida's rule through the institutionalization of some form of military-civilian diarchy.

The most controversial proposal of all, which calls for a "government of national consensus," has met with strident opposition from both the government and the leaders of the two parties. Popularized in December 1991 by a group of 13 previously banned and detained politicians, including seven who had been state governors under the Second Republic, this proposal seeks to address the problems of national integration, democratic consolidation, and economic reconstruction by prescribing the effective involvement of all the political parties, plus a wide spectrum of influential nonpartisan constituencies, in the governance of the Federation. In this regard, the proposal echoes the late Murtala Mohammed's 1975 argument that Nigeria's future constitution should "discourage institutionalized opposition to the government in power and, instead, develop consensus politics and government based on a community of all interests rather than the interest of sections of the country."[11]

Several proponents of a government of national consensus have directly impugned the legitimacy and viability of Babangida's transition program by linking their proposal to calls for the convening of a "national conference" like those held in several other West and Central African countries in recent years. Such a conference, it is hoped, could negotiate the outlines of a national consensus on the prickly issues of federal structure, the party system, presidentialism, revenue-sharing, and the relationship between religion and the state.

Legitimate questions may be raised about the wisdom and appropriateness in present circumstances of schemes for government by an all-embracing coalition or a national conference. Yet the idea of "consensus politics" usefully underlines the need for the political class to achieve a crucial modicum of agreement on basic values like the rule of law, political moderation and accountability, free and fair elections, and interethnic fairness. Indeed, without such agreement, it is difficult to be optimistic about even the short-term prospects for federal democracy in Nigeria.

Political Reform and Economic Reform

The peculiarities, irregularities, and tensions that vex Nigerian federalism stem in part from the rule of the generals. For some 23 of its 33 years of independence, Nigeria has been governed by centralizing, authoritarian military elites who seized power after corrupt and inept politicians flagrantly abused constitutional and electoral procedures. Under military rule, Nigerian federalism has suffered not only from excessive centralization and from the turmoil engendered by arbitrary acts of ethnic and religious animosity, but also from the lack of a climate conducive to learning and bargaining, constitutional adaptation, and consensus-building among the political class.

In the final analysis, however, the institution of a stable democratic system of civilian rule will probably not take place, or contribute significantly to the strengthening of the federal system, without appropriate reforms in the country's political economy. The coherence of the federalist project in Nigeria and the development of peaceable interethnic relations have been undermined by what President Babangida calls a "cake-sharing psychosis" that would reduce the nation's oil-based economy to a "financial conduit" designed purely to channel riches to sectional elites and their constituents.[12] The increasingly frenzied struggles for federal "political power in order to preside over the sharing-out of the painlessly derived oil largesse" and the structurally debilitating pressures to create new states and local government areas represent perhaps the worst expressions of this syndrome.[13]

In spite of all of this, however, Nigeria has made remarkable progress since the onset of military rule toward instituting a relatively functional federal system. What is more, there can be little doubt that the intractable difficulties likely to ensue from an attempt to repeal this system would be far more costly than expending the creative energies needed to reform it. If the country's leaders can find ways to promote interethnic justice, nurture a sense of political moderation and fair play, and broaden opportunities for groups and individuals, Nigeria's search for an order that is enduring, truly federal, and truly democratic may yet reach a successful conclusion.

The search for a more viable federal system must focus not only on the diversification of the country's economic base, but also on revenue-sharing reforms that could reduce the incentives for establishing new states and localities. For instance, a revenue-sharing scheme that decreases the emphasis on interunit equality, more fairly rewards the major contributors to national wealth, and compels all constituent units to raise half of their revenues internally, may go a long way toward quelling the clamor for new states and local governments while also redressing some of the grievances of the oil-producing areas.

Nigeria's leaders must also continue to experiment with strategies for balancing, distributing, and rotating power among various groups. Both the "federal character" principle and its informal expression within the party system (i.e., "zoning") have become established as constructive policies for ethnic power-sharing in Nigeria. Care must be taken, however, to ensure that these policies do not simply legitimize or reproduce the hegemony of the bigger nationalities, or ignore important nonethnic cleavages in Nigerian society. Indeed, the careful incorporation of these nonethnic forces into the dynamics of power-sharing may help to mitigate much of the exaggerated sectionalism that many critics see in the current theory and practice of federalism.

Moreover, there is a need to defuse regional resentment of the continuing use of the "federal character" principle to promote affirmative action in education and the bureaucracy. Nigeria's affirmative action policies are designed mainly to benefit not a weak minority, but the politically dominant, if educationally disadvantaged, north. Recently, the federal government rejected its own commission's recommendation that such practices be phased out by the year 2000. A federal program to expand and improve educational opportunities in the north would be far less invidious and contentious than the current policy of affirmative action, which most southerners perceive as divisive, restrictive, and politically motivated.

Lastly, recent events underscore the wisdom of devising institutions that can induce a modicum of harmony among the members of the political class. The absence of such a consensus was most recently demonstrated by the failure of the politicians to unite behind the SDP

and Moshood Abiola in the wake of Babangida's June 1993 assault on
the democratic process, an attack that has suddenly opened up a new
phase of potentially ruinous polarization and anxiety in the country. The
crucial challenge is to devise structures that can give every segment of
the civilian political class a stake in the fledgling democratic process.
This may require more than just the accommodation of the political
opposition and various regional interests in the national government.
Rather, it should also involve the diffusion of many powers and
resources that presently are concentrated in the federal government in
general, and in the federal presidency in particular. By lowering the
intensity of struggles for control of the central government, and by
expanding opportunities for self-governance at state and local levels,
such decentralization could greatly encourage the practice of genuine
democracy and authentic federalism in Nigeria.

NOTES

1. Larry Diamond, "Nigeria: Pluralism, Statism, and the Struggle for Democracy," in
Larry Diamond, Juan Linz, and Seymour Martin Lipset, eds., *Democracy in Developing
Countries: Africa* (Boulder, Colo.: Lynne Rienner, 1988), 65.

2. Brian Smith, "Federal-State Relations in Nigeria," *African Affairs* 80 (1981): 373.

3. *Nigerian Tribune* (Ibadan), 24 September 1992, 1.

4. Ken Saro-Wiwa, "Federalism and the Minority," *The Guardian,* 30 November 1992,
37.

5. Ibid.

6. *The Guardian,* 22 January 1992, 2.

7. Daniel Bach, "Managing a Plural Society: The Boomerang Effects of Nigerian
Federalism," *Journal of Commonwealth and Comparative Politics* 27 (1989): 234.

8. Olusegun Obasanjo, "The Nigerian Society and the Third Republic," *The Guardian,*
14 March 1992, 9.

9. Balarabe Musa in *Citizen* (Kaduna), 29 March 1993, 12.

10. See Federal Republic of Nigeria, *Report of the Political Bureau* (Lagos: Federal
Government Printer, 1987), 75-76.

11. "Address by the Head of the Federal Military Government at the Opening Session
of the Constitution Drafting Committee on 18 October 1975," in *Constitution of the
Federal Republic of Nigeria 1979* (Kaduna: New Nigerian Newspapers, 1981 reprint), 124.

12. "Text of 1992 Budget Address by President Babangida," *National Concord,* 1
January 1992, 111. The reference to the oil economy as a "financial conduit" is from C.S.
Whitaker, "The Unfinished State of Nigeria," in Richard Sklar and C.S. Whitaker, *African
Politics and Problems in Development* (Boulder, Colo.: Lynne Rienner, 1991), 269. See
also Richard Joseph, "Class, State and Prebendal Politics in Nigeria," *Journal of
Commonwealth and Comparative Politics* 21 (1983): 21-38.

13. Izoma P.C. Asiodu, "The Political Economy of Fiscal Federalism," *Daily Times,*
19 February 1993, 19, 36. See also Ladipo Adamolekun and John Kincaid, "The Federal
Solution: Assessment and Prognosis for Nigeria and Africa," *Publius: The Journal of
Federalism* 21 (Fall 1991): 173-88.

5.
INDIA: THE DILEMMAS OF DIVERSITY

Robert L. Hardgrave, Jr.

Robert L. Hardgrave, Jr. *is the Temple Professor of the Humanities in Government and Asian Studies at the University of Texas, Austin. His numerous publications include* India Under Pressure *(1984) and (with Stanley A. Kochanek)* India: Government and Politics in a Developing Nation *(5th ed., 1993).*

India came to independence in 1947 amidst the trauma of partition. The nationalist movement, led by Mohandas K. Gandhi and Jawaharlal Nehru, aimed to gather what was then British India plus the 562 princely states under British paramountcy into a secular and democratic state. But Mohammad Ali Jinnah, leader of the Muslim League, feared that his coreligionists, who made up almost a quarter of the subcontinent's population, would find themselves a permanent and embattled minority in a Hindu-dominated land. For Jinnah, India was "two nations," Hindu and Muslim, and he was determined that Muslims should secure protection in an Islamic state of Pakistan, made up of the Muslim-majority areas of India. In the violence that accompanied partition, some half a million people were killed, while upwards of 11 million Hindus and Muslims crossed the newly created borders as refugees. But even all this bloodshed and suffering did not settle matters, for the creation of Pakistan left nearly half of the subcontinent's Muslims in India.

Muslims today are India's largest religious minority, accounting for 11 percent of the total population. Among other religious groups, the Sikhs, some of whom in 1947 had sought an independent Sikhistan, are concentrated in the northern state of Punjab and number less than 2 percent of India's population. Christians, Buddhists, Jains, Parsees, and Jews add further richness to India's religious diversity, but their comparatively small numbers only accentuate the overwhelming proportion of Hindus, with some 83 percent of the population.

The Hindus, although they share a common religious tradition, are themselves divided into a myriad of sects and are socially segmented by thousands of castes and subcastes, hierarchically ranked according to tradition and regionally organized. The geographic regions of India are linguistically and culturally distinct. There are more than a dozen major languages, grouped into those of Dravidian South India and Indo-European (or Aryan) North India; Hindi, an Indo-European language spoken by 30 percent of all Indians, is recognized by the Constitution of 1950 as the official language (along with English). In addition to the many Indo-European and Dravidian languages and dialects, there are various tribal languages spoken by peoples across India, most notably in southern Bihar and in the seven states of the Northeast.

In confronting this staggering diversity, the framers of India's Constitution sought to shape an overarching *Indian* identity even as they acknowledged the reality of pluralism by guaranteeing fundamental rights, in some cases through specific provisions for the protection of minorities. These include freedom of religion (Articles 25-28); the right of any section of citizens to use and conserve their "distinct language, script or culture" (Article 29); and the right of "all minorities, whether based on religion or language," to establish and administer educational institutions of their choice (Article 30). With respect to caste, the Constitution declared the practice of "untouchability" unlawful (Article 17). To provide compensatory justice and open up opportunity, a certain percentage of admissions to colleges and universities and places in government employment were "reserved" for so-called Scheduled Castes (untouchables) and Scheduled (aboriginal) Tribes (Article 335). Similarly, to ensure adequate political representation, Scheduled Castes and Tribes were allotted reserved seats in the Lok Sabha, the lower house of Parliament, and in state legislatures in proportion to their numbers (Article 330). These reservations were to have ended in 1960, but they have been extended by constitutional amendment at ten-year intervals.

Federalism and the Party System

Despite enormous pressures, India has been remarkably successful in accommodating cultural diversity and managing ethnic conflict through democratic institutions. This success has in large part been the product of that diversity itself, for at the national level—what Indians call "the center"—no single ethnic group can dominate. Each of the 25 states in India's federal system reflects a dominant ethnolinguistic group, but these groups are in turn divided by caste, sect, religion, and a host of socioeconomic cleavages. Federalism provides a venue, however flawed, for expressions of cultural distinctiveness, but it also serves to compartmentalize friction. The cultural conflicts of one state rarely spill over into another, and the center can thus more effectively manage and contain them.

Even as India reflects a multitude of cross-cutting identities, however, religion has the potential to shape a national majority. Political appeals on the basis of pan-Hindu identity, facilitated by modern mass communications, have begun to forge an increasingly self-conscious religious community capable of transcending its own heterogeneity. The expression of this communal awareness as Hindu nationalism poses a fundamental challenge to India as a secular state.

India's party system, like its constitutional framework, has served to sustain democratic politics and national unity, providing access to political participation for newly mobilized groups. For 41 of the 46 years since 1947, India has been governed at the center by the Indian National Congress, the party that led India to independence. For the first two decades after independence, the main arena of political competition at both national and state levels was within the Congress party, but with increasing frequency since the mid-1960's, regional parties have successfully challenged Congress's hold on various states. Then in 1977, opposition parties for the first time defeated Congress at the center.

Today there are three major forces at the center, represented by parties that at least claim to be "national" in character. The Congress, under Prime Minister P.V. Narasimha Rao, rules as a minority government sustained by its alliances with an array of minor and regional parties. The Congress draws its support widely from across the country, from all classes and groups, but a critical margin of support has traditionally come from religious minorities, notably Muslims, and from untouchables. The leading opposition party is the Bharatiya Janata Party (BJP), the party of Hindu nationalism. From its base in the Hindi-speaking heartland of North India, it has dramatically expanded its support by direct appeals to pan-Hindu religious sentiment. Though its strength is still concentrated in the north, the BJP has made inroads, especially among the urban middle classes, into other parts of India.[1] The third force at the center is made up of various Janata Dal (People's Party) factions that draw support principally from the rural peasant classes, mainly in North India, and the Left Front, led by the Communist Party (Marxist), the ruling party of West Bengal.

The Congress remains the only genuinely all-India party, for the other claimants for power at the center have bases of support that are largely confined to particular regions. Any party or coalition that wishes to rule at the national level, however, must represent a range of cultural identities. Even the BJP, in seeking to forge a Hindu nation, must cast its net broadly—though in doing so, it excludes Muslims and other minorities unwilling to subordinate their distinctive identities.

At the state level, national parties compete with those that are wholly regional in their base of support, and in a number of states, regional parties—identified with particular ethnic, linguistic, or religious groups—are the major political forces. In the southern state of Tamil Nadu, for instance, Tamil nationalist parties have ruled since 1967; in Andhra Pradesh, the Telugu Desam party is the major rival to the Congress; in the Punjab, it is the Sikh party, known as the Akali Dal; and in the Northeast, ethnically based regional parties compete with Congress in various states. Ethnically or religiously based parties serve as vehicles of regional identity within a united India, but can also threaten cultural minorities by wielding nativist appeals to local "sons of the soil" whose interests are supposedly being endangered by migrants from other parts of India or indigenous religious and linguistic minorities. Such appeals dramatically expose the tensions that lie just under the multicultural surface of Indian democracy.

Liberal democracy stands or falls according to its ability to elicit a dual commitment to *both* majority rule *and* minority rights. The legitimacy of a majority at any given time depends on the maintenance of an open marketplace of ideas, free and periodic elections through which the majority can be challenged, and guarantees of basic human rights for all. But how and in what form are minority rights to be protected? Liberal democracy is classically expressed in terms of individual rights, and the Preamble to the Indian Constitution embodies a commitment to justice, liberty, equality, and fraternity for the individual. Yet minority interests are typically expressed in terms of *group* identity, and political demands may call for the protection or promotion of language, religion, and culture, or of the "group" more generally, in ways that conflict not only with "the will of the majority," but with constitutional guarantees of individual rights and equal protection. This tension, and the problems it causes, can be seen in India in the contexts of: (1) ethnolinguistic regionalism and separatism; (2) caste-based reservations; and (3) secularism and Hindu-Muslim communal relations.[2]

Regionalism and Separatism

With independence, the old princely states were integrated into the Indian union, but the newly created federal states were linguistically and culturally heterogeneous. Long before independence, the Congress party had organized its provincial branches along linguistic lines, and demands for the reorganization of states on a linguistic basis brought the issue before the Constituent Assembly. Nehru and the Congress leadership feared that linguistic states would have a "subnational bias" that would retard national integration and unleash "fissiparous tendencies." Moreover, they argued, most states, however their boundaries might be drawn, would still have linguistic minorities. But the democratic logic behind the call for linguistic states—the notion that state administration and judicial processes should be conducted in the language of the local

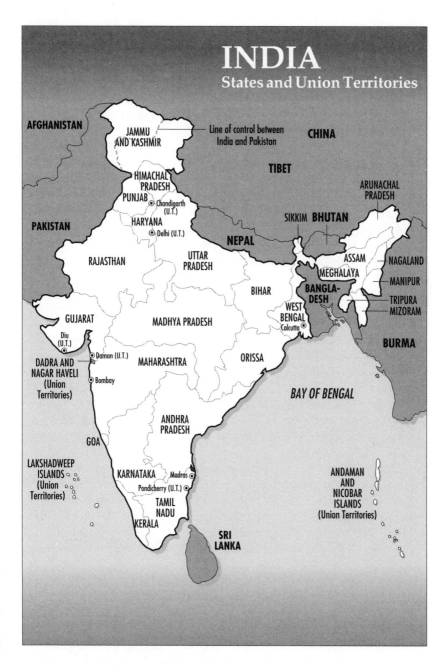

INDIA
States and Union Territories

AFGHANISTAN

JAMMU AND KASHMIR

Line of control between India and Pakistan

CHINA

TIBET

HIMACHAL PRADESH

PUNJAB

Chandigarth (U.T.)

ARUNACHAL PRADESH

PAKISTAN

HARYANA

Delhi (U.T.)

SIKKIM BHUTAN

NEPAL

RAJASTHAN

UTTAR PRADESH

ASSAM NAGALAND

MEGHALAYA

MANIPUR

BIHAR

BANGLA-DESH

WEST BENGAL

TRIPURA
MIZORAM

Calcutta

GUJARAT

MADHYA PRADESH

BURMA

Diu (U.T.)

Daman (U.T.)

DADRA AND NAGAR HAVELI (Union Territories)

Bombay

MAHARASHTRA

ORISSA

BAY OF BENGAL

ANDHRA PRADESH

GOA

LAKSHADWEEP ISLANDS (Union Territories)

KARNATAKA

Madras

Pondicherry (U.T.)

ANDAMAN AND NICOBAR ISLANDS (Union Territories)

TAMIL NADU

KERALA

SRI LANKA

From Robert L. Hardgrave, Jr. and Stanley A. Kochanek, *India: Government and Politics in a Developing Nation*, 5th ed. (Fort Worth, Texas: Harcourt Brace Jovanovich, 1993).

majority—was compelling. Political pressure for the reorganization of states ultimately proved irresistible. Beginning in 1953 with the creation of Andhra Pradesh as a Telugu-speaking state, and then in 1956, with a more general reorganization on a linguistic basis, the principle of language as the basis for state boundaries was broadly accepted.

The federal reorganization of 1956, however, did not quell demands for the creation of new states. In 1960, following widespread agitation and violence, the state of Bombay was bifurcated to form the linguistic states of Maharashtra and Gujarat; in 1966, the Sikhs secured a Punjab state; and in the following years, several tribal states were carved out of the Northeast. In 1987, India's twenty-fifth state was created as the former Portuguese colonial enclave of Goa was elevated to statehood. The pressures continue today. In the late 1980s, Nepalis in West Bengal's Darjeeling district raised the demand for a separate "Gurkhaland" state within India. After two years of violence, in which more than 300 people were killed, the Gurkha National Liberation Front accepted a proposal for what would be, in effect, an autonomous region within the state of West Bengal; lately, however, it has renewed its demand for a separate Gurkha state. The Bodo tribals of Assam have pursued a violent struggle—thus far unsuccessfully—for the creation of a separate Bodoland. More formidable is the demand by tribals in mineral-rich southern Bihar and the contiguous districts of neighboring states for a Jharkhand state. This demand has been voiced with varying intensity since 1947, but in 1992 it reemerged with new militancy, as strikes and bombings were directed to an economic blockade of the region.

The organization of states on a linguistic basis provides the framework for expanded political participation. It permits people more effective access to government—but with the drawback that their use of this access may all too often reflect the parochialism of language and region. The creation of linguistic states has reinforced regionalism and stimulated demands for increased state autonomy. India's Constitution guarantees freedom of movement with only a few qualifications, yet almost every state outside the Hindi heartland of central India has spawned a militant nativist movement directed against outsiders. The fundamental issue has been employment for local people, and many state governments, either officially or unofficially, have supported the protection of jobs for the "sons of the soil." Among the most virulent is the Shiv Sena, a regional party in Maharashtra. Exploiting local grievances and economic frustration, the Shiv Sena, under the banner "Maharashtra for the Maharashtrians," has directed both verbal and physical attacks at South Indian immigrants and Muslims.

In the Northeast, the issue for the Assamese is not only jobs, but the preservation of the Assamese language and culture in the face of a demographic shift that threatens to make the Assamese a minority in their own state. Bengalis have been migrating into Assam for more than a century, but since 1971, the influx of "foreigners" (Bengali Muslims from Bangladesh) has deepened ethnic insecurity and served as the catalyst for a movement that engulfed Assam in violence. In a six-year-long agitation (1980-86), more than five thousand people were killed in ethnic conflict. In 1986, the government of Prime Minister Rajiv Gandhi reached a settlement with the movement leaders. By the terms of the accord, the central government promised—in addition to commitments for the deportation of illegal immigrants and enhanced economic development—to provide "legislative and administrative safeguards to protect the cultural, social, and linguistic identity and heritage" of the Assamese people.

Assam's agony did not end with the accord, which is still largely unfulfilled; like other states in the ethnically turbulent Northeast, it continues to suffer from violent convulsions. In the tribal states of Nagaland and Mizoram, India has fought against insurgency movements since 1947, and among the tribal peoples of the Northeast more generally, the aspiration for independence from India has been met by a renewed Indian determination to secure the territorial integrity of the union.

India is a federal system with a strong central government. The Constitution also lists state and concurrent powers, but provides the center with a capacity to intervene in state affairs and even to dismiss elected state governments and impose its own authority through "President's Rule." Under Prime Minister Indira Gandhi (1966-77; 1980-84), centralization of power increased dramatically, both within government and in the structure and operation of the ruling Congress party. The results were an increasing, almost pathological, imbalance in the relationship between the center and the states and growing demands for autonomy voiced by non-Hindi states. In Tamil Nadu, for example, anger at the status of Hindi as the national language was the catalyst for the rise to power of ethnoregional parties; similar discontent was seen in Andhra, resulting in the victory of the Telugu Desam party; and in West Bengal, where the Communist Party (Marxist) functions as a regional party. Most notable, however, is the Punjab, where in 1982 the Sikh-dominated Akali Dal pushed demands for greater state autonomy and Sikh militants launched a campaign of terrorism for an independent nation of Khalistan.

Punjab and Kashmir

No "ethnic" conflict in India has been more traumatic than the one involving the Punjab, "homeland" of the Sikhs, who make up some 55 to 60 percent of the local population. At least twenty thousand people have died in political violence there since 1981. The state has been under President's Rule for long periods marked by draconian methods of keeping order.[3] This has nurtured mutual distrust between Hindus and Sikhs, and official actions like the army's June 1984 incursion into Amritsar's Golden Temple, the major Sikh shrine, alienated most Sikhs from the government, if not from India itself. It was in revenge for the violation of the temple that two Sikh members of her own bodyguard murdered Prime Minister Indira Gandhi in October 1984. While tensions originally developed over nonsectarian demands behind which all Punjabis, Hindu and Sikh, could rally, the Akali Dal set these issues in the context of various demands for the protection of Sikh religious interests that excluded Hindus and to which the central government, affirming its commitment to secularism, would not yield. For the militants challenging the Akali Dal for Sikh leadership, this refusal proved that the Sikh religion could be protected only by an independent, theocratic Sikh state. For the Akalis, the issue was political power; for the militants, it was (or so they claimed) Sikh identity itself and the fear of absorption into the Hindu majority.

Aggrieved though they were, most Sikhs in the Punjab opposed the idea of Khalistan, and by the late 1980s, the original political and religious goals of many terrorist gangs had been displaced by the routinization of extortion, robbery, and murder as a way of life. The people, sickened by both terrorism and police repression, were ready for a return of the political process. After 56 months of direct rule from New Delhi, state-assembly elections were held in February 1992. Under terrorist threat and Akali Dal boycott, a low voter turnout brought a Sikh-led Congress government to power. Initially enjoying little credibility, the government won increasing popular confidence, and in the village-council elections of January 1993, with terrorists quiescent, 82 percent of the electorate turned out. With the restoration of self-government and the continued police campaign against the militants, the Punjab crisis eased—though the specter of terrorism remains to haunt any return to normalcy.

In the far-northern state of Kashmir, India faces an even more serious problem. India and Pakistan have fought two wars over what was once the princedom of Jammu and Kashmir, which remains the principal source of antagonism between the two nations. For India, the state—now divided by a "line of control"—is fully a part of the Indian union; with its 65-percent Muslim population, it stands as a symbolic rebuttal to the "two nation" theory that underlay the founding of Pakistan. Moreover, India asserts that Kashmir's inclusion in India serves as a guarantor of the secular state. Pakistan, on the other hand, continues to insist that the people of Kashmir be allowed to decide by plebiscite whether to be a part of India or Pakistan—a demand that rests on the assumption that the decision would be for Pakistan. The largest number of the state's Muslims, however, would likely choose an independent Kashmir, and this has been the goal of the Jammu and Kashmir Liberation Front (JKLF), albeit with comparatively little popular support before 1988.

Hindus predominate in Jammu, and Tibetan Buddhists in the sparsely populated region of Ladakh; it is only in Kashmir proper that Muslims form a majority, but at 4 million they account for but a small portion of India's more than 100 million Muslims. Under the National Conference, as the regional Muslim party of Jammu and Kashmir is called, the state had been comparatively quiet, but in the late 1980s more and more Kashmiri Muslims—increasingly alienated by fraudulent elections, widespread corruption, and the failure of the center to help their state develop economically—responded to the nationalist call for the liberation of Kashmir from "Hindu India." In 1988, the JKLF and an assortment of separatist and fundamentalist groups initiated a wave of strikes, bombings, and assassinations. Imposing President's Rule, the center responded with what Pakistan, Kashmiri Muslims, and Indian human rights advocates decried as an indiscriminate use of force, further alienating the people of Kashmir.

The principal groups involved in the Kashmir insurgency are the Jammu and Kashmir Liberation Front, which supports an independent and secular Kashmir, and the Islamic fundamentalist Hezb-ul-Mujahideen, which is closely linked to Pakistan's Jammiat-i-Islami party and the presumed recipient of Pakistani largess. The sources of the separatist movement are internal to Kashmir and owe their origin to years of maladministration at home and political interference from New Delhi, but the agitation has had support from within Pakistan. Some 250,000 troops of the Indian Army and paramilitary forces are deployed in Kashmir, but their inability to suppress the uprising underscores the limits of force when, as here, it is unaccompanied by a political process that effectively engages at least those few prepared to enter into dialogue. But with Kashmiri moderates so often targeted for assassination, and with a death toll of 12,000 and rising in all political violence since 1989, prospects for a settlement are dim.

India's federal system once acted to compartmentalize social unrest, with political crises often containable within a single state or region. But the centralization of power also centralized problems, bringing to the desk of the prime minister issues once resolved at the state level. The balance must be restored through a devolution of power to the states, indeed, perhaps to an increased number of states and possibly "autonomous regions" within states. But this devolution must be accompanied by the constitutional guarantee of civil rights and liberties to ensure that all persons receive the equal protection of the law. Among the many measures proposed for redressing the balance between the center and the states, the most compelling include an end to the arbitrary dismissal of state governments and imposition of President's

Rule; a more equitable sharing of revenues; and a respect by the center for spheres of public policy that are properly state concerns.[4]

Caste Reservations

Hindu society in India is divided by caste and subcaste in a complex hierarchy that stretches down from Brahmins to untouchables. The 1950 Constitution abolished untouchability and specified that no citizen be subject to any disability or restriction with regard to places of public use or accommodation on the basis of caste. Political representation was guaranteed for Scheduled Castes (untouchables) and Tribes through the proportionate reservation of seats in elected legislative bodies, from Parliament to village councils. But despite these various provisions and the extended protections of the Untouchability (Offenses) Act, untouchables—who today number more than 130 million—continue to suffer discrimination and deprivation. To address this situation and to overcome the cumulative results of past discrimination, the government instituted a program of "compensatory discrimination"—an Indian version of affirmative action—that reserved 22.5 percent of all central-government jobs for members of Scheduled Castes and Tribes. Comparable reservations were provided for state-level employment, and reservations were extended to college and university admissions.

The system has been controversial, and many higher-caste Hindus, particularly Brahmins, who have been denied government employment or entrance into universities, feel that they have been victims of reverse discrimination. Far more controversial, however, has been the extension of reservations to "Other Backward Classes"—specific castes chosen because of their low levels of social and educational advancement. Predominantly rural, they account for a substantial portion of India's population and in many states command significant political power. In response to that power, a number of states have extended reservations in university admissions and government employment to them.

In 1980, the Backward Classes Commission, chaired by B.P. Mandal—a former chief minister of Bihar state and himself a member of a backward caste—recommended the reservation of 27 percent of all central government jobs for the backward classes in addition to the 22.5 percent already reserved for the Scheduled Castes and Tribes. The 3,743 castes and subcastes identified as beneficiaries make up 52 percent of the Indian population. The report gathered dust for a decade, but in 1990, then-Prime Minister V.P. Singh announced that his Janata Dal government would implement the Mandal recommendations. The decision brought widespread criticism from the press and strong opposition from higher castes, especially students. In New Delhi and other cities in the north of India, violent protests (including self-immolations) and shootings by police raised the specter of "caste war."

Singh declared the reservations a matter of social justice, but to his political opponents, it was seen as a cynical political move to shore up his threatened base of support among the backward peasant castes. Given the numbers involved, however, no political party could oppose the reservations outright, although the left argued for reservations based on income and educational criteria rather than upon caste. Implementation was stayed by the Supreme Court, pending a ruling on the constitutionality of the measure. Returned to power in 1991, the Congress party under Prime Minister P.V. Narasimha Rao sought to mollify opposition to the reservations by adding a 10-percent reservation for the poor of the higher castes. In November 1992, the Supreme Court upheld the reservation for backward castes, with the provision that it be need-based, but struck down the additional 10 percent as constitutionally impermissible. The complexities of the court decision effectively preclude implementation of the reservation, but the controversy has sharpened caste enmities.

Rather than leading India toward a "casteless" society, the policy of reservation has reinforced caste identities. Reservations for untouchables may indeed be compelling because it is precisely their *caste* identity that has been the source of stigma and discrimination, but in using caste rather than individual need as the criterion for benefits, their identity *as* untouchables is officially sanctioned. Moreover, the dilemma is manifest in that all untouchables do not benefit equally. Reservations go disproportionately to the more "advanced" among the untouchables, while those most in need remain effectively excluded.

The "backward" castes share with the untouchables a comparatively low level of educational and social advancement, but their position is not the result of discrimination based on caste, nor do they suffer the stigma and disabilities associated with untouchability. And for all their "backwardness" as a group, they command considerable political power and, as peasants, many among them enjoy increasing prosperity. It is thus very hard to justify reservations for the backward castes: the appropriate response is to individual need and merit, not group identity.

Hindu-Muslim Conflict

India may be an officially secular state, but Indian society is defined by religious identities and riven by communal mistrust and hatreds. In India, the term "communal" refers principally to Hindu-Muslim conflict, and with memories of partition still bitterly nurtured, Hindu-Muslim tensions are sustained by jealousy and fear. Each year several hundred incidents of communal violence and rioting are officially reported, and their number and intensity have grown in recent years. In December 1992, following the destruction of the mosque at Ayodhya by Hindu fanatics, rioting across the country left some 1,200 persons dead. In

January 1993, Bombay witnessed a nine-day anti-Muslim pogrom that left more than six hundred people dead.

Since the early 1980s, the rise of Muslim fundamentalism in India has spurred a heightened Hindu consciousness and led Hindu nationalists to project India's 83-percent Hindu majority as threatened. Hindu nationalism has its roots in the late nineteenth century and is today represented by an increasingly formidable range of organizations and parties—the powerful paramilitary Rashtriya Swayamsevak Sangh (RSS), its revivalist affiliate Vishwa Hindu Parishad (VHP), and the Bharatiya Janata Party (BJP), the leading opposition political party with ambitions to take control of the central government. With visions of a revitalized Hindu India, they portray India's secularism as no more than a pretext for the "pampering" of religious minorities.

Secularism in India does not erect a "wall of separation" between church and state, but rather seeks to recognize and foster all religious communities. The Constitution guarantees freedom of worship and the right of each religious group to establish and administer its own schools and to maintain its distinct traditions. But in India, as in the United States, the form and degree of state accommodation of religious practice have been matters of controversy. At issue is the appropriate democratic balance between majority preference and minority protection.

In the wake of partition and the heightened insecurity of India's remaining Muslim population, the Congress government under Nehru permitted Muslims to retain their personal law (governing such matters as marriage, divorce, and inheritance) while amalgamating other Indians under a uniform civil code. For Hindu nationalists, who would recognize no exceptions, this smacked of a "pseudosecularism" that privileged Muslims over Hindus. The issue was dramatically confronted in the 1985 Shah Bano case. The Supreme Court had ruled in favor of a 73-year-old woman, Shah Bano, divorced after 43 years of marriage by her husband in the traditional Muslim manner, and awarded her a monthly maintenance from her husband, where Muslim personal law would have required none. Muslim clerics, with the cry of "Islam in danger," rallied Muslims to the cause and warned that imposition of a uniform civil code would deny them the right to follow the injunctions of their faith.

In an attempt to stem the loss of Muslim support from the Congress party, Prime Minister Rajiv Gandhi (initially favorable to the judgment) announced support for the Muslim Women (Protection of Rights on Divorce) Bill that would remove Muslim divorce from provisions of law and, in effect, scuttle the Supreme Court decision. Though welcomed by traditional Muslims, the bill came under immediate attack by progressive Muslims, women, secularists, and Hindu chauvinists. Hindus are not disadvantaged by the application of Muslim personal law, although Muslim women may surely enjoy fewer rights than their Hindu sisters. But this was not a human rights issue for Hindu nationalists, to whom the government's response to the Shah Bano case simply demonstrated the appeasement of minorities they had long denounced. In pandering to Muslims, Hindu nationalists declared, the Congress party had sold out the Hindus and their birthright as rulers of India.

Hindu nationalists project a mythic Hindu majority that denies the diversity that makes Hinduism—and India—what it is. They have invented a muscular Hinduism that would, through the state, impose a conformity as oppressive to the individual Hindu as to the recalcitrant minority. Religion, for the Hindu nationalists, is the vehicle by which they seek to achieve political power and restore Ram-rajya, the ideal rule of the mythic age of Lord Ram. The conceptual catalyst is Hindutva ("Hinduness") a term that embodies the notion that all Indians—including Muslims—are part of a Hindu nation and that Ram and the gods and heroes of Hindu mythology are part of their patrimony. Those unwilling to accept Hindutva are thus not just apostates but traitors.

The god Ram is the potent symbol that Hindu nationalists have chosen to weld Hindus, disparate in their profusion of sects and traditions, into a self-conscious community. The city of Ayodhya in Uttar Pradesh is the presumed birthplace of Lord Ram, and devotees assert that in the sixteenth century the Mogul emperor Babur destroyed the temple marking the birthplace and in its place constructed a mosque, the Babri Masjid. In 1989, efforts by the Vishwa Hindu Parishad and other Hindu revivalist groups to demolish the Babri Masjid and "to recapture injured Hindu pride" through the construction of a new temple of Ram precipitated what was up to that time probably the most serious Hindu-Muslim rioting since partition in 1947. In 1990, to galvanize Hindu sentiment behind the BJP, party president L.K. Advani launched his *rath yatra* (chariot pilgrimage), a 10,000-kilometer journey in a van fashioned to look like a mythological chariot across the heart of North India to Ayodhya to launch the construction of the new temple. Prime Minister V.P. Singh, invoking the principles of secularism, warned that the mosque would be protected "at all costs." As Advani and other BJP leaders approached Ayodhya, they were arrested. The BJP, in turn, withdrew its parliamentary support from the minority Singh government, and after an unprecedented 346-to-142 vote of no-confidence on November 5, the prime minister submitted his resignation.

In the fall of 1992, the VHP and BJP vowed that on December 6, they would begin building a new temple at the sacred site. More than 200,000 Hindu militants converged on Ayodhya and at the appointed hour stormed through the police barricades and demolished the Muslim shrine. The police and paramilitary guarding the mosque offered little resistance. In face of the action and subsequent rioting, the Congress government of P.V. Narasimha Rao seemed paralyzed; when the prime minister finally did act, he dismissed the BJP government of Uttar

Pradesh, India's most populous state, and imposed President's Rule. A week later, the governments of the remaining three BJP-ruled states were dismissed. Advani and other Hindu-nationalist leaders were arrested and charged with inciting the militants. The central government also announced two-year bans on three Hindu communal organizations—the RSS, VHP, and the fascistic Bajrang Dal—as well as two Muslim fundamentalist groups. The president of the VHP vowed that any government efforts to impede the construction of the new Ram temple would result in "a confrontation of unimaginable magnitude."

As Hindu-Muslim antipathies intensify, India's secularism finds itself increasingly challenged at every level of society, from the drawing rooms of New Delhi intellectuals and the rising urban "consumer" middle class to the ranks of saffron-clad VHP militants and the armed thugs of the Bajrang Dal and the Shiv Sena. The challenge is to India as a secular state and to its capacity to secure democracy, justice, and equality in a multicultural society.

Majority Rule and Minority Rights

India's experience enables us to draw some conclusions about the democratic management of ethnic and religious conflict:

• Democratic conflict management requires a substantive distribution of power between the center and the periphery and among the various groups within the country. A balance must be maintained between steps taken to check tendencies toward the overcentralization of political power and steps taken to contain the centrifugal forces that can rip apart a multicultural state.

• There is also a tension between the liberal emphasis on individual rights and the assertion of group rights and identity, and the democratic polity must find its way toward balance here as well.

• Historically, problems of ethnic and religious conflict in India have eased when political and group leaders have sought to deal with them through accommodation, bargaining, and the political process, and particularly when the center has sought accommodation with minority groups. Problems tend to get worse when the center intervenes directly to impose an outcome on a group or region asserting its independent interests and identity. Force alone has been unable to overcome separatist tendencies; if it is to be successfully applied, it must be accompanied by political dialogue and accommodation.

In every democracy, there is necessarily a tension between majority rule and minority rights, yet the two are by the same token inextricably bound together. Indeed, democracy is sustained because there is no single, monolithic, and permanent majority, but rather a shifting series of ruling coalitions made up of minorities. The minorities may reflect the cross-cutting social cleavages and overlapping memberships that characterize the idealized model of democratic pluralism, or else may form a mosaic of distinct groups that define their identity in terms of one or more attributes like religion, language, or caste. In either event, there must be an underlying political culture of mutual respect and trust or, at a minimum, a basic agreement on the rules of the political game among the various groups themselves. Lacking such a consensus, one group, or perhaps a coalition, may seek power and domination over others; if the center cannot hold, the society may find itself torn apart by war and secession.

In India, in a political culture of mutual distrust and increasing violence, the dangers are legion. India's democracy is challenged by communalism, excessive caste consciousness, and separatism. But in the state response to these challenges, India confronts yet another dilemma—weakening the very values of individual liberty that are at the core of its democratic commitment. In its attempts to quell endemic unrest and the challenge of terrorism, India has enacted a plethora of laws that have become instruments of repression; police and paramilitary abuses seem to get worse while all sorts of other violations of human rights are reported with numbing frequency. But for all the challenges, pressures, and dilemmas to which India is exposed by virtue of its plight as a multicultural state, Indian democracy, sustained through ten elections, still shows remarkable strength and resilience.

NOTES

1. The growth of the BJP is reflected in its increase in seats in the Lok Sabha, India's lower house of Parliament—from 2 seats won in 1984 (7.4 percent of the vote) to 85 seats (11.4 percent) in 1989, and, contesting twice as many seats as in earlier elections, 119 seats (21 percent) in 1991.

2. For an extended discussion of these issue areas, with extensive bibliographic references, see Robert L. Hardgrave, Jr. and Stanley A. Kochanek, *India: Government and Politics in a Developing Nation*, 5th ed. (Fort Worth, Texas: Harcourt Brace Jovanovich, 1993), especially ch. 4, "The Challenge of Federalism," 125-66, and ch. 5, "Arenas of Conflict: Groups in Indian Politics," 167-215.

3. Provisions for designated "disturbed areas" permit arrest and detention without trial for as long as two years; secret trials by special tribunals; and wide powers of censorship. For a discussion of the array of such laws, see ibid., 209-12.

4. The 1988 *Sarkaria Commission Report on Center-State Relations* made a number of recommendations that would enhance "cooperative federalism," but its measured proposals have been largely ignored.

6.
CANADA: FROM BILINGUALISM TO MULTICULTURALISM

Hugh Donald Forbes

Hugh Donald Forbes *teaches political science at the University of Toronto. The author of* Nationalism, Ethnocentrism and Personality *(1985), he has recently completed a book on ethnic conflict, and is currently working on a study of the sources of multiculturalism.*

Mass migration has created Canada's problems of ethnic conflict and accommodation, as it has those of the United States. From the seventeenth century to the present, large numbers of Europeans have migrated to the New World, displacing its aboriginal inhabitants and thus creating a more or less cohesive native or indigenous minority. Migrants from Africa and Asia—forced in the past, voluntary more recently—have added other ethnic minorities distinguished by "visible" or "racial" differences. The numerically dominant European population is itself, of course, ethnically divided—in the Canadian case, primarily between the English and the French, but secondarily between the older migrants from Northern Europe and the more recent "New Canadians" from Southern and Eastern Europe.

Canada's parliamentary democratic institutions have been successful so far at managing the tensions associated with these divisions, and Canadians are rightly proud of their success. Indeed, one common purpose or ambition of Canadians—beyond simply consuming the fruits of the highest technology applied to the most abundant natural resources—is to show the world how to manage ethnic conflict, so as to avoid the horrors of the past century. But Canada's status as a model of skillful management is threatened by the growing racial tensions in Canada's large cities and by the separatist movement among French-speakers in Quebec. To understand the lessons that Canada may have to teach, one must begin by noting the historical and institutional background to the current situation.

The golden age of ethnic accommodation in Canada lasted a little over a century, from the 1840s to the 1950s. The most important division during this period, as more recently, was the division between English and French.

Modern Canada is the result of the sudden, trans-Atlantic imperial expansion of the British and French peoples, resulting in a series of clashes between their empires throughout the seventeenth and eighteenth centuries. Canada took form as a result of "The Conquest" (of the French by British forces under General James Wolfe in 1759) and then the northward migration of British Loyalists who opposed the American Revolution two decades later. Two groups of colonists, one English-speaking and Protestant, the other French-speaking and Roman Catholic, but both defined in part by their opposition to the American colonists to the south, came together under the sovereignty of the British Crown.

The nature of British rule in Canada—its monarchical and confessional character—was at odds with the liberal and democratic tendencies of the age. The Catholic clergy in Quebec and the Tory Loyalists and officials elsewhere checked these tendencies for a time, but no such feeble dikes could long withstand the flood.

The Rebellions of 1837 marked the end of the attempt to give the Canadian colonies "balanced" constitutions with established churches. An investigation was conducted by a leading British politician, Lord Durham, whose report advocated "responsible government" (i.e., local democratic self-government within a quasi-federal imperial structure) and "assimilation" (i.e., the absorption of the French population within a commercial society of a modern English or American character).

In the Province of Canada (meaning what are now Ontario and Quebec), responsible government was achieved in 1848 by an alliance between English and French "moderate reformers" who rejected "assimilation" by restoring the official use of French in the legislature. Over the following decade, these politicians and others like them worked out practical arrangements—with respect to the sharing of power, the role of the churches, landholding, schools and universities—that are still the basis for Canadian life. They relied upon two main devices, federalism and "brokerage" (or multiethnic) parties, to overcome English-French rivalry.

Even before the drafting and adoption of a written federal constitution (the British North America Act of 1867), they practiced an informal federalism involving dual ministries and separate legislation for the English-Protestant and French-Catholic parts of a formally united province. In 1867, the enactment of Confederation divided Canada into Ontario and Quebec and joined these new provinces to the Maritime Provinces and British Columbia, under a written federal division of powers. Canada counts its birthdays from 1867, but from the perspective of central Canada, that year has about the same significance as 1789 (rather than 1776) in American history: it was more a confirmation and consolidation than a "founding."

Table 1 — Home Language by Province, 1991

HOME LANGUAGE	QUEBEC	NEW BRUNSWICK	REST OF CANADA	TOTAL
English	11%	68%	88%	68%
French	83	31	2	23
Other	6	1	10	9
(Total =)	(6.8M)	(0.7M)	(19.5M)	(27.0M)

SOURCE: Statistics Canada, *Home Language and Mother Tongue*, 1991 Census of Canada, Catalogue Number 93-317, Table 1.

The social (or geopolitical) basis for Canadian federalism has been the vastness of the country and the location and concentration of French-speakers within it. Quebec and New Brunswick have been their homelands, where they constitute an overwhelming majority and a substantial minority, respectively. Outside of these two provinces, the French have always been few in number—about 2 percent of the population in the most recent census, judging by the language respondents reported using at home (see Table 1). Only in the so-called "bilingual belt" (a band running roughly from Sudbury, Ontario, through Ottawa and Montreal into the Eastern Townships, with an extension in the Acadian part of New Brunswick) have the two populations met in large numbers on a daily basis.

The geographical separation of the two populations has encouraged the development of "two solitudes" socially and "brokerage" or "elite accommodation" politically. The first important multiethnic party was the midnineteenth-century alliance of "moderate reformers" mentioned above. It was followed by the Liberal-Conservative party of John A. Macdonald and George Etienne Cartier, which was the heart of the "great coalition" that brought about Confederation. The Progressive Conservative party now in power is descended from it. Why did such parties develop and take root? There is no discounting the importance of particular leaders, but there were also favorable circumstances, including the internal divisions within both the English and French communities. For many years both were deeply divided by questions of democracy and authority, so that each of the conflicting groups tended to look to the other community for political allies.

Ethnic conflict did not disappear during the "golden age." The French nursed their grievances as a conquered and oppressed minority—but prospered and reproduced nonetheless. The English took quiet (sometimes not so quiet) pride in their status as conquerors whose Empire was carrying "the white man's burden" of civilizing "backward races." But their own religious diversity, and the rough balance of forces in the country as a whole, encouraged tolerance and accommodation. Tempers flared from time to time over issues having to do with the Church in Quebec (the Jesuit Estates problem); the settlement of the Western territories (the Riel Rebellions and the Manitoba and North-West schools questions); and Canadian participation in Great Britain's wars (the conscription crises). But never in this period did English-French conflict seriously threaten lives, property, or the existence of the country.

How is this success to be explained? Several conditions, in addition to those associated with federalism and brokerage, deserve brief mention. Relative numbers, for example, have been important: both the English and the French populations have grown rapidly (the former mainly through immigration and assimilation, the latter through natural increase), but the ratio between them remained stable at about 2 to 1 for most of the period in question. The differences between the two groups have always involved language, laws, religion, history, and culture or education, but until recently the religious difference was generally considered most important, and it was kept out of politics (more or less) by certain basic similarities between the English and French populations as well as by a liberal policy of neutrality. More generally, the liberalism of the period before World War II meant a small, "negative" state with limited social responsibilities, and therefore not much for the two groups to quarrel about that the government controlled directly. A common enemy—the Americans—kept them aware of their value to each other. The prestige of the United Kingdom, when it was at the zenith of its power, appeased French resentment about having been conquered and made it easier for English Canadians to be generous.

Finally, it seems clear that the rejection of "assimilation" in the 1840s and earlier was a key to peaceful relations between the English and the French. Assimilation is admittedly hard to define, and it is unclear exactly what Durham meant when he used the term, but it was profoundly threatening and offensive to French Canadians. No doubt many English Canadians have looked forward to the eventual absorption of the French within a vast English-speaking throng, but most have avoided talking openly about "assimilation." The politicians learned early to conduct their relations on the assumption that both "races" are permanent features of the universe, like the sun and the moon. Had they not done so, there is little reason to believe that Canada, as a country uniting English and French territories, would exist today.

The Challenge of Separatism

A new phase of English-French relations began a little over a generation ago with the election of a Conservative federal government that lacked strong support in Quebec and then a Liberal provincial government in Quebec dedicated to reform. "Separatism," whose roots can be traced as far back in French-Canadian history as one wants, began to be widely discussed, and "nationalism" changed its character. Language displaced religion in the definition of the French-Canadian "race." Social progress, not salvation, became its goal. Nationalists no longer spoke of their compatriots as a minority, "French Canadians," who were dispersed across the country and whose "minority rights" needed protection, but rather as a majority, les Québécois, exploited by foreign capitalists and oppressed by Anglo-American cultural imperialism. Feared by businessmen, this new French-Canadian nationalism evoked considerable sympathy from English Canadian journalists and intellectuals, though perhaps more in Toronto than in Montreal.

It was a time of rapid social change. Television, the pill, and mass foreign travel were undermining the old social order. Immigration was changing the character of Canada's large cities, and in Montreal in particular, there were some bitter confrontations between immigrants, who wanted their children schooled in English, and the French. (A rapidly falling birthrate among the French made the linguistic assimilation of immigrants more important than it had been in the past.) Anticolonialism abroad and the civil rights movement in the United States gave Quebeckers (and Canadians generally) a model of nationalism not tainted by Hitler.

French Canadians in Quebec, it soon became plain, would no longer accept just being "tolerated" on their provincial "reserve." Some, who called themselves Québécois, wanted indépendance so that they could be a "normal society" with a French majority and progressive social policies. Others defended federalism, but on the condition that it better recognize the equality of French and English, despite their unequal numbers. By the time of Canada's centenary in 1967, these two options, égalité ou indépendance, had come to dominate politics in Quebec.

Since the early 1960s, the problem of Quebec separatism has dominated federal politics as well. The federal government's basic response to it was fixed in 1963 by the appointment of a royal commission "to inquire into and report upon the existing state of bilingualism and biculturalism in Canada and to recommend what steps should be taken to develop the Canadian Confederation on the basis of an equal partnership between the two founding races . . ." The language was archaic, but the basic idea was new: equality of English and French to be symbolized by the equal status of the English and French languages in federal government institutions, as well as by equal support for the cultural activities of English and French Canadians.

Pierre Elliott Trudeau, who became Canada's prime minister at the head of the Liberal Party in 1968, represented in his own person and lineage the ideals of bilingualism and biculturalism. In 1969 his government passed an Official Languages Act, which made Canada "officially bilingual." The Act aimed to defuse separatism by elevating the status of French, and thus of French Canadians, within the federal government. It affirmed the right of all Canadians to receive services from the federal government "in the official language of their choice." To provide these services, bilingual civil servants had to be hired (the Act was a kind of affirmative action program for French Canadians) and unilingual ones had to be made bilingual (for the better part of a decade, many civil servants, most of them "anglophones," spent many hours a week attending language classes).

While Canada was becoming more bilingual, however, Quebec was becoming less so. The separatist forces in Quebec had been united in 1968 behind a new provincial party, the Parti Québécois (PQ), with an ambiguous platform, "sovereignty-association," and an attractive leader, René Lévesque. The PQ came to power in Quebec in 1976, and the following year it passed its own "official languages act," the Charte de la Langue Française, which lowered the official status of English in Quebec.[1]

The PQ had won power on a promise to hold a referendum on independence before trying to declare it. In 1980 the referendum was held, and the sovereignty option clearly lost, with only 40 percent of Quebeckers favoring it, as against 60 percent opposed. No one will ever know what exactly would have happened had the PQ won its referendum—what kind of negotiations about "sovereignty" and "association" would have ensued—but one thing was clear by 1980: the political class of English Canada had decided to abide by the results of such a referendum. If most Quebeckers wanted independence, better to let them have it than to use force to try to keep Quebec within the federal structure. In fact, of course, the federalists won the referendum, and separatism vanished from the political agenda.

The Issue of Constitutional Reform

In the struggle against it, Trudeau had given Quebeckers "bilingualism" and he had promised them "constitutional reform": it was to be their reward for voting *non*. But the amendments eventually adopted were not at all what a succession of Quebec provincial governments, federalist as well as separatist, had been demanding for 20 years. In 1982, Trudeau succeeded in entrenching a Charter of Rights and Freedoms in the constitution, greatly increasing the scope for judicial review by the federally appointed judiciary and thus limiting the powers of both the federal and provincial governments. Indeed, Sections 2 and 23 of this Charter began the process of vetoing important parts of Quebec's Charte de la Langue Française. The government of Quebec (still in the hands of the PQ) had refused to approve the proposed amendments, but after some legal and political wrangling, it had been decided that their approval was not required.

Trudeau's Charter has been a surprising popular success in English Canada. It appeals to individualist and populist sentiments as well as to belief in expertise. Many Canadians evidently regard judges not just as legal oracles, but as tribunes of the people.

The reaction of Quebec's French Canadians is harder to describe. Individualism, populism, and belief in expertise are undoubtedly important among them as well, but they tend to see the Charter of Rights as something that Trudeau and English Canada have imposed on Quebec, and which shifts power to the federal government. According to the view represented by Trudeau, this should not be a problem. Since Quebec never really had a veto, it could not be deprived of one, and the Québécois would gradually forget the anger they felt upon suddenly discovering this lack in 1982, if the politicians would cease stirring the embers of their resentment. The problem is that political gains can be made by appealing to Quebec's injured pride. This was shown in the federal election of 1984 and more recently by the sudden rise since 1990 of a new separatist *federal* party, the Bloc Québécois.

In 1984 Brian Mulroney, a bilingual Quebecker of Irish descent at the head of the federal Conservative Party, managed to win most of Quebec's seats (and thus a huge majority in the House of Commons) by promising further constitutional amendments that would restore Quebec's veto and win its formal approval of the changes made in 1982. Between 1987 and 1990 he came extremely close to resolving the problem (and perhaps creating further problems, as his critics contended) through a package of amendments known as "the Meech Lake accord." This package won the enthusiastic support of the government of Quebec (now Liberal and federalist), but it required the approval of all the other provincial legislatures within three years, and both Newfoundland and Manitoba (in keeping with broad popular sentiment) chose to demur.

The failure of Meech Lake in mid-1990 brought the separatist movement in Quebec back to life and seemed to leave Canada on the brink of dissolution. Over the next two years, a frantic process of intergovernmental negotiations and popular consultations produced "the Charlottetown agreement," a bloated, ill-defined package of proposed constitutional and other amendments which, among other things, recognized that Canada's native peoples have an "inherent right of self-government." The agreement was put to Canadians for approval in principle in a series of referenda in October 1992, but despite a massive propaganda campaign by business and government, it was decisively rejected, both in Quebec ("not enough for Quebec") and in the rest of Canada ("too much for Quebec").

The summer of 1993 finds Canada in a kind of interregnum. Few seem content with "the constitution," but all are tired of talking about it. The economy is mired in the worst depression since the 1930s. The Conservatives in Ottawa have been setting record lows in the polls, but they have a bright new leader in British Columbia's Kim Campbell. A federal election must be held this fall. With three or four important parties competing in almost every (single-member simple plurality) constituency, only the politicians are claiming to know who will emerge victorious.

Multiculturalism

Canada's problems of ethnic conflict and accommodation have been discussed so far as if all Canadians were either English or French and as if the only real problem of Canadian politics were the relation between these two groups. Such assumptions are at best half truths. In fact, Canadians of British and French origin represent only about two-thirds of the total Canadian population, and Canada's multiculturalism may be far more important, as a contribution to political theory or the political arts, than anything connected with its dualism.

Canada's population has more or less doubled every 40 years since Confederation. In the early decades, most of the growth due to immigration was the result of immigration from the British Isles. At the turn of the century, immigrants from other European countries began to arrive in significant numbers, and during the 20 years following World War II, they counted for about six of every ten immigrants to Canada. For the past 20 years, however, Asia has been the most important source of immigrants, with significant numbers also coming from Africa and the Caribbean. These flows explain not just the appearance of "visible minorities" in Canada's cities, but a relative decline of the "two founding races" and a growing predominance of English over French. These changes are the most important factors conditioning Canada's recent ethnic politics.

Precise statistics on ethnicity are difficult to compile, since many people do not fit simple ethnic categories.[2] Many are the products of marriages that leave them with no clear ethnic identity, or with one they wish to shed. Ethnicity is like much else: people often think of themselves quite differently from how they are thought of by others. An ethnic-origin census of the Canadian population at the present time would, however, reveal a breakdown like the following:[3] British 37 percent, French 27 percent, Other Europeans 25 percent, Asians and Africans 8 percent, and Native Peoples 3 percent. Clearly the "Other European" "third force" is now almost as large as the French component of the population, and the old 2 to 1 ratio of English to French is either not attained or greatly exceeded, depending upon how all the "others" are classified. A good reason for considering most of them "English" is apparent from the census statistics on language. If all those who report speaking English at home are compared with those who report speaking French, the ratio is now about 3 to 1 (see Table 1 above).

The political significance of the changes under way first became apparent a generation ago, with the appointment of the Royal Commission on Bilingualism and Biculturalism mentioned above. Many Canadians objected to the basic idea of "bilingualism and biculturalism": if this dualism were carried to its logical conclusion, they argued, then the English and the French would acquire a special status in Canada, and the other ethnic groups would be relegated to "second-class citizenship." The government of the day, sensitive to this objection, directed the commission to recommend measures "to develop the Canadian Confederation on the basis of an equal partnership between the two founding races," but with the crucial qualification, "taking into account the contribution made by the other ethnic groups to the cultural enrichment of Canada and the measures that should be taken to safeguard that contribution." Two of the ten commissioners it appointed were "ethnic" Canadians (i.e., of neither British nor French ethnic origin).

In 1971 Prime Minister Trudeau, responding on behalf of his government to the publication of the fourth volume of the commission's report (which dealt with "The Cultural Contribution of the Other Ethnic Groups"), read into it a compromise that the commissioners themselves had been unable to agree upon: two official languages, but no official cultures, with all cultures to be treated equally in so far as culture can be separated from language and from the maintenance of the overall Canadian way of life, which was not in question. The key passage in his brief statement to the House of Commons was:

> It was the view of the royal commission, shared by the government and, I am sure, by all Canadians, that there cannot be one cultural policy for Canadians of British and French origin, another for the original peoples and yet a third for all others. For although there are two official languages, there is no official culture, nor does any ethnic group take precedence over any other. No citizen or group of citizens is other than Canadian, and all should be treated fairly.[4]

This historic compromise ("multiculturalism within a bilingual framework") entailed a patchwork of new policies. Some were designed to encourage cultural retention by minority ethnic groups (i.e., to inhibit or oppose assimilation); others, which promoted contact and opposed discrimination, aimed to encourage social integration (despite its tendency to increase assimilation); and still others tried to hasten linguistic assimilation by subsidizing the learning of the official languages by recent immigrants.

Official "multiculturalism," despite its suffix, does not refer to any coherent theory or set of principles. Rather, the term denotes a hodgepodge of policies and practices. It is, in a sense, just the application to the other ethnic groups of the basic approach taken so far in dealing with French-English conflict: uphold individual rights; avoid talking about "assimilation," except to decry it; and find ways of symbolizing the equality of numerically unequal groups, without abandoning majority rule. The only real principle discernible underneath all this is that of liberal tolerance or neutrality. Neutrality must now be achieved, however, by a "positive" state, not by keeping "hands off" the social or cultural sphere, but by putting "hands on" (through posters, subsidies, grants, human rights commissions, employment equity programs, broadcasting licenses, and the like) in a fair or equal way.

Multiculturalism has been embraced by most English-speaking Canadians, not just by those whose status was boosted by the proclamation of their equality to the "founding races." The reasons for this are a bit difficult to discern, for they involve both noble motives and others less readily avowed. Generally speaking, Canadians wish to set a good example regarding the just accommodation of ethnic differences in the "global village." By virtue of their history, they are inclined to adopt an approach ("the mosaic") that differs slightly from that of their southern neighbors ("the melting pot"). In recent years, heavy immigration from "nontraditional sources" has been providing the raw materials for a social experiment to test the superiority of the Canadian approach. This immigration has tended to boost the price of urban land and reduce labor costs, which has added to its appeal, and that of multiculturalism, for important segments of the population. As well, the experiment satisfies (at least temporarily) the longstanding Canadian desire to be different from the United States—to be a distinct society with better customs and values. In 1971, multiculturalism appealed to a common tendency and desire to see Canada as a more "European" country than the United States—more progressive, socialist, tolerant, diverse, stylish, and sophisticated (as Trudeau was more "European" than President Nixon).

Multiculturalism appeals to the common understanding of freedom as choice. The architects of multiculturalism appear to have envisioned a society in which individuals would be free to be whatever they wanted to be culturally. They would not be expected to adhere to the customs and values of their own ethnic group, nor would they feel any pressure to conform to those of the majority. They would not suffer discrimination at the hands of the dominant group (or groups) because of their cultural traits (apart from language and education), nor would they be vulnerable to the antipathy of their ethnic compatriots for failing to adhere to their ancestral traditions. They would be free to practice their own culture or to deviate from it and practice that of another group—or to "mix and match"—with only their own individual preferences to guide them. Ethnicity and culture, traditionally regarded as matters of fate, would become matters of choice.

Official multiculturalism, like the immigration policies that underlie it, is a long-range policy with delayed effects. Opinion about it may change as the public becomes more aware of the full scope of the diversity hidden under the term "culture" and the difficulties likely to be encountered trying to protect and enhance individual rights while proclaiming equal respect for all cultures.

One immediate practical effect of multiculturalism has been to complicate English-French relations. The principle that all ethnic groups are equal clashes with the principle that the two largest are; the French, as the weaker of the two large groups, detect in the proclaimed equality of all a demotion in status. For reasons already indicated, French Canadians tend to prefer a "bicultural" to a "multicultural" definition of Canada, though their opposition to the latter tends to be expressed cautiously, since the values or ideals of multiculturalism (diversity, peace, nondiscrimination, etc.) are embraced as wholeheartedly by French as by English Canadians.[5] Opposition tends to be expressed as support for Quebec's independence, or by asking why the English should not be on the same footing as, say, the Chinese in a multicultural Quebec, rather than the French enjoying equality with the Ukrainians and Jamaicans in a multicultural Canada?

On the English side of Canadian society, multiculturalism provides a new rationale for old complaints about Quebec's retrogressive and xenophobic tendencies, as became clear in the controversies surrounding the Meech Lake and Charlottetown accords. Ethnic Canadians tended to oppose Quebec's demands, but more importantly, their presence and official status meant that English Canadians generally could in good conscience, for the best of motives, oppose concessions that would have the effect of elevating French Canadians above other minorities. By what right, many asked, should French Canadians (or Quebec) be any more equal (or "distinct") than any other ethnic group (or province)? Some reasoned that the French-English problem, given its deep historical roots, must belong to a former age; new Canadians have no interest in these old quarrels, which will gradually fade away as the number of Canadians who are neither English nor French, and who have other priorities, increases.

The Native Peoples

The most interesting of the groups whose status is affected by official multiculturalism are the native peoples. They represent only a small fraction of the Canadian population, but their numbers have been growing rapidly in recent decades. A century ago there were only about

100,000 Canadian Indians, Métis (people of mixed Indian and European blood), and Inuit, and most of them lived in remote areas. Today there are considerably more than half a million, and many have migrated to the large cities of southern Canada. In the past their most serious problems were the threats to their health from malnutrition and the infectious diseases brought by Europeans; today they suffer from the destruction of their traditional ways of life and the violence, diseases, and accidents associated with alcohol abuse. Long marginalized because of the alleged inferiority of their "primitive" cultures, they now have powerful ammunition in their struggle for equality.

The native peoples differ from other oppressed or marginalized minorities because of their attachment to the land and their status as its first occupants. The territories rightly theirs have not, however, been clearly defined by treaties or legislation. Twenty years ago a complicated process for resolving conflicting land claims was begun; it will require at least another twenty years for its completion. Not just in the far north, but in southern Canada as well, huge tracts of land are in dispute, and it is no longer clear by what right the ancestors of today's "white" Canadians occupied the "New World" generations ago.[6]

One particularly ominous development has been growing uncertainty about the real boundaries of Quebec, should it attempt (following a victory by the separatist PQ) to declare its independence. At the time of the referendum in 1980, Canada's political class was agreed that "Quebec" meant the territory shown on the maps used in schools and sold in service stations. But arguments can be made both for expanding Quebec's territory greatly (for example, by incorporating Labrador) and for contracting it even more drastically (by returning it to its boundaries of 1898 or 1867). Quebec's old dispute with Newfoundland over Labrador is dormant. The issue has not been formally resolved, but serious claims are unlikely to be made in any foreseeable future. Contraction is another matter. In recent years, maps showing the province's old boundaries have received significant attention in the English-Canadian media. And because of Quebec's poor relations with the native peoples on its present territory, Quebec's separation from Canada might well trigger a process by which the native peoples in the North try to separate from the newly independent nation, in order to remain part of Canada. How the relevant governments—including the American—would react in such a situation is impossible to predict.

The Canadian Dilemma

For more than two hundred years, peaceful and reasonably friendly relations have been maintained between the English and the French in Canada, despite their traditional rivalry and their religious and linguistic differences. Only one reason for this modest success bears repetition.

The politically dominant group, the English, have always shrunk from "assimilation" as a way of dealing with the French. Many of them have no doubt hoped that "society" would eventually produce a uniformity of language and culture that "the state" dared not try to impose, but their leaders have always publicly recognized ethnic diversity.

The conditions for the accommodation of English and French have, of course, changed as the scale of economic life has grown, as new groups have appeared, as population has shifted from the countryside to the cities, as great corporations and bureaucracies have come into being, and as ideas of cultural equality and national liberation have gained adherents. The language policies adopted by the federal and Quebec governments in the 1960s and 1970s were responses to these changing conditions. Perhaps neither of them was the right response.[7] It is also possible, though more difficult, to argue that both were appropriate.

In 1971 Pierre Trudeau applied the putative lessons of Canada's English-French experience to the new problems posed by the growing numbers and political importance of "ethnic" Canadians. At first his "official multiculturalism" was just a slogan and a hope—a political gambit embodied in a patchwork of minor policies that had little practical effect. The relevant groups were European minorities whose cultures did not differ profoundly from the common culture of English and French Canadians, and whose numbers, actually and potentially, were small. Their religious differences, which paralleled those of English and French Canadians, had already been accommodated. The rhetoric of multiculturalism, extreme as it may have sounded, referred only to elusive and somewhat trivialized "identities" symbolized by differences in crafts, cuisine, and folkdancing.

It is another matter to employ the same rhetoric in a context of rapidly growing "Third World" minorities and an increasingly restive native population. Canadians have hardly begun the daunting business of thinking through what cultural equality might mean beyond the realm of the innocuously folkloric—with respect to serious questions surrounding dress, education, employment, family law (or customs), foreign policy, genital modifications, gerrymandering, jury selection, medical care, and public holidays, for example.

Many Canadians are now uneasy about the apparent implications of multiculturalism in this new context. They wonder if their country might have bitten off more than it can chew by encouraging immigration while abjuring assimilation. Would it not be wiser, they ask, to put more emphasis on common values and the *Canadian* identity? The difficulty is to spell out those common values that define the Canadian identity—without invoking multiculturalism. Canada has no founding documents that proclaim familiar, universally valid truths. The country has always had a more "ethnic" character than the United States. It began as a union of British and French, and it now seems committed to searching for *its* universally valid truths where perhaps none are to be found, in the portentous but vague rhetoric of ethnic accommodation.

Perhaps future Canadians will look back on the past 20 or 30 years as the dawn of a new golden age of accommodation in which Canadians, despite their growing differences of race, religion, language, culture, and ancestry, learned to deal fairly and sensitively with each other as parts of a multicultural "just society." Canada's success so far has bred a certain complacency among most of her people. If we succeeded in the past, they ask, why not in the future? But the conditions that facilitated accommodation in the past have pretty much disappeared, and the country faces new and more complex challenges.

> *"...the conditions that facilitated accommodation in the past have pretty much disappeared, and the country faces new and more complex challenges."*

Ethnic diversity no longer has a clear territorial pattern. Most of it is in the cities, where people of widely different backgrounds live in close proximity to one another. Racism is now more important than religious intolerance, though the occasions for the latter form of bigotry have certainly not disappeared. Federalism is no longer as clear a remedy for conflict as it used to be. Indeed, by giving power to local majorities, as against widely dispersed but sizeable minorities, federalism may just add to the problems of accommodation.

Trudeau's 1982 Charter of Rights has given ethnic accommodation a legal dimension, making it the business of judges. Perhaps it will benefit from their prestige, though it may suffer from their rhetoric of rights and their natural tendency to take a legalistic approach to political problems. "Whatever judges may lack in political astuteness or suppleness," one may surmise Trudeau thought, "they are better insulated than politicians from majority passions and they have more authority, so the compromises they impose are more likely to be accepted." It is a theory that will be tested with the passing of time.

Canada's multiethnic "brokerage" parties are in difficulty. They are challenged externally by new parties—such as Reform in the West and the Bloc Québécois in Quebec—that make no pretense of trying to bridge English-French (or any other important ethnic) differences. Internally, they have been weakened by a growing number of bitter "nomination fights": rivals for a party's nomination mobilize their own ethnic compatriots to pack the local nomination meeting, and the result is an unseemly clash of ethnic groups. Regardless of who wins, the party (as broker) loses. Tinkering with the electoral system in order to introduce an element of proportional representation might temporarily help to alleviate these difficulties, but in the long run it might only aggravate them by encouraging the growth of small, ethnically exclusive parties.

The political scene is now changing in Canada. Campaigning has begun for the upcoming federal election. For the next several months, questions of leadership and the economy promise to dominate political discussion. Kim Campbell seems to be having some success restoring the Conservative party's popularity, but in Quebec, support for the Bloc Québécois remains strong. The election, while it will undoubtedly have a cathartic effect in the country, may produce a stalemate in Ottawa and (for the first time) a significant separatist presence in the House of Commons. The government of Quebec is also approaching the end of its mandate. Its premier, Robert Bourassa, is in poor health. His Liberal party, which has defended federalism in Quebec for the past 25 years, has nonetheless alienated much of its anglophone support, and it could split between nationalists and federalists in the attempt to choose his successor. Practical politicians must try to predict the unpredictable; academic observers can note the long-term decline in the commitment of Canadians to federalism and English-French brokerage, as other problems of ethnic accommodation have become more pressing.

NOTES

I wish to thank Stefan Dupré for his comments on an earlier version of this essay. Any remaining errors of fact or judgment are mine alone.

1. Three years earlier, Bill 22, a somewhat less stringent and provocative language law, had been passed by the previous Liberal government under Robert Bourassa. It made Quebec "officially unilingual" and required the children of immigrants to attend French schools.

2. If Canada's population grows as fast in the next 60 years as it has in the past 120, and if most of the increase is due to immigration, and if most of the immigrants come from Asia, then about half the Canadian population will be Asian by the middle of the next century. Current projections anticipate lower rates of population growth, but there is no good reason—given Canada's empty spaces and the power of capitalism to create jobs—why it should not be higher. The political support for increased immigration from any source tends to grow with the numbers from that source. Cf. Economic Council of Canada, *Economic and Social Impacts of Immigration* (Ottawa: Supply and Services Canada, 1991), and Daniel Stoffman, *Toward a More Realistic Immigration Policy for Canada* (Montreal: C. D. Howe Institute, 1993).

3. The following statistics have been compiled from the responses to the ethnic origin question in the 1991 census, which allowed multiple responses, including "Canadian." Statistics Canada, *Ethnic Origin*, 1991 Census of Canada, Catalogue 93-315 (Ottawa: Industry, Science and Technology Canada, 1993), Tables 1A and 2A. Respondents who gave multiple responses have been distributed among the simpler categories according to the relative frequencies of such responses.

4. Trudeau's short speech and a longer document which was tabled at the same time ("Federal Government's Response to Book IV of the Report of the Royal Commission on Bilingualism and Biculturalism") are in House of Commons, *Debates*, 1971, VIII, 8545-46 and 8580-85. Trudeau's speech is reprinted in Howard Palmer, ed. *Immigration and the Rise of Multiculturalism* (Toronto: Copp Clark, 1975), 135-37, and in H.D. Forbes, ed. *Canadian Political Thought* (Toronto: Oxford University Press, 1985), 349-51.

5. Quebec, like several of the other provinces, has an official multiculturalism of its own. The difficulty, as explained by a leading Canadian social scientist, is that multiculturalism involves "a rewriting of Canadian history," and such "symbolic innovations" generally require a reallocation of status among social groups. "This reallocation is itself a source of tension and conflict which needs to be managed if the eventual result is not to be the opposite of what is desired." Raymond Breton, "Multiculturalism and Canadian Nation-Building," in Alan Cairns and Cynthia Williams, eds., *The Politics of Gender, Ethnicity and Language*, Macdonald Commission Studies No. 34 (Toronto: University of Toronto Press, 1986), 61-2. Cf. Economic Council of Canada, *Economic and Social Impacts of Immigration*, 115 and 125: "The climate of public opinion in Quebec differs from that in the other provinces. . . . [The recognition that Quebec could not assimilate into its traditional culture all the immigrants it believes are needed for its economic development] did not come easily to the majority of Francophones in Quebec, many of whom believe that being a Quebecker requires support for, and affirmation of, the French culture."

6. A current dispute in the courts (*Delgamuukw v. The Queen*) involves ownership and jurisdiction over 58,000 square kilometers of northwestern British Columbia—an area three times greater than Massachusetts, almost twice as large as Belgium, or 50 percent greater than Switzerland. Algonquin Park, a tract of land more than twice the size of Rhode Island and just a couple of hours north of Toronto, is the focus of another dispute. Hundreds of smaller disputes, some involving slivers of land no bigger than Manhattan, are also being decided.

7. For a clear presentation of a sensible case against Trudeau's policy of official bilingualism, see Kenneth McRoberts, "Making Canada Bilingual: Illusions and Delusions of Federal Language Policy," in David P. Shugarman and Reg Whitaker, eds., *Federalism and Political Community: Essays in Honour of Donald Smiley* (Peterborough: Broadview Press, 1989).

7.
THE FATE OF MINORITIES
IN EASTERN EUROPE

Janusz Bugajski

Janusz Bugajski, *a former senior research analyst at Radio Free Europe in Munich, is associate director of East European studies at the Center for Strategic and International Studies in Washington, D.C. He has just completed a book entitled* Ethnic Politics in Eastern Europe: A Guide to Nationality Policies, Organizations, and Parties, *which will be published by M.E. Sharpe later this year.*

After four decades of statist centralism and "socialist internationalism," a far-reaching ethnic reawakening has accompanied the disintegration of communist rule and the collapse of multinational federations in Eastern Europe. Virtually all states there have been wracked by ethnic and regionalist movements demanding some degree of political self-determination, a role in national decision making, and a more equitable distribution of economic resources. Both majority and minority populations have been affected by this rebirth of ethnicity, and in some instances the aspirations of different communities have clashed, resulting in conflicts that threaten to derail the progress of democratic reform.

Ethnic nationalism may be a positive or a negative phenomenon: it can be aggressive or defensive, rational or emotional, consistent or unpredictable; it has moments of intensity, periods of passivity, and it is often contradictory. On the positive side, ethnic nationalism may be a cohesive and motivating force in helping a group to assert its cultural identity, regain its national sovereignty, or limit the influence of unwelcome outside powers in domestic affairs. Nationalism may instill a sense of patriotism, community loyalty, and cultural pride. During wrenching periods of revolutionary change, shared ethnicity—with all its mythic, ritualistic, and symbolic ingredients—may provide an important anchor of continuity and stability.

Nationalism becomes a negative force if and when it takes on a pronounced ethnocentric bias, asserting the superiority of one group's culture, language, and religion and excluding various alien elements in order to strengthen the solidarity of the ethnic community. Operating on the axiom that a perceived domestic or foreign threat helps to unite a community, aggressive nationalist leaders promote discrimination against other nationalities and hostility toward neighboring states. The persecution of minorities by newly independent nations may also be a form of aggressive compensation for prior oppression at the hands of foreign elites, or defensiveness based on exaggerated fears of domination, absorption, or extinction. Xenophobic nationalism is more likely to be manifested among groups that live with larger and potentially more threatening minorities, especially where there are deep-rooted historical grievances and seemingly irreconcilable cultural or religious differences. Numerous issues can provoke hostility and confrontation, including questions of land ownership, language policy, and the allocation of power and resources.

> *"Governments and political movements may seek to manipulate nationalism for either defensive or offensive purposes."*

The growth of ethnocentrism usually stimulates a nationalist response among neighboring groups, often for purposes of self-protection. Recently revived nationalism can be vibrant and confident without being chauvinistic, or it may breed paranoia and foster the growth of ethnic or religious differentiation and communal conflict.

Governments and political movements may seek to manipulate nationalism for either defensive or offensive purposes. By fostering isolationism, nationalism can delay progress toward international integration. Moreover, if political life is organized according to ethnic criteria, power may become polarized with little opportunity for compromise, the alternation in power of competing political elites, or the participation of minority parties in decision making.

Eastern Europe has a long history of irredentist and secessionist movements. Some states have from time to time fomented such movements in order to promote instability among neighbors, often en route to annexation. The danger persists that almost every manifestation of even nonseparatist ethnic aspiration among minorities, especially when backed by outside powers, can be interpreted as proof of deliberate subversion. If left unchecked, pressures for minority rights could be seen to challenge central control over a minority region, or even to threaten the disintegration of the state.

The existence of ethnic or cultural minorities resistant to assimilation can become a serious obstacle to nation-building or state integration, especially if such minorities claim some form of political autonomy. This can arouse the ire of the majority, fueling intercommunal conflict and possibly generating repression in the form of forced assimilation or expulsion of minority groups. Such developments can in turn transform moderate minority autonomists into radical separatists. Southeastern Europe in particular has a poor record when it comes to protecting minorities, giving outside powers an excuse to press for territorial revisions and annexations. This is where the term "Balkanization" originates, signifying persistent interethnic clashes and territorial competition resulting in a spiral of international instability.

Demands for minority rights can be divided into two kinds that may be difficult to reconcile. First is the right to fully equal opportunities in access to education, economic resources, cultural facilities, and political institutions, along with the elimination of discrimination based on ethnicity, race, culture, or religion. Second is the right to special protection, preferential access to certain resources, and positive discrimination by way of government funding to promote minority cultures. Either of these two "rights" can foster resentment among the majority population or among minorities not favored by government policy. Minority nationalism may be a valuable lever for community mobilization and for gaining political influence. Conversely, the withholding of political and economic resources from minority leaders can aggravate anticentrist feelings, strengthen the cohesion of ethnic minorities against the adversarial state, undermine the legitimacy of the government, and lead to ever more radical demands. Pressures for ethnic autonomy may then evolve beyond the protection of cultural identity and accelerate toward demands for outright separation.

"Autonomy" may be cultural or political. Cultural autonomy implies control by an ethnic group over its own educational institutions, mass media, and various social and cultural activities. Political autonomy is more far-reaching, involving every aspect of social, economic, and administrative life short of national defense and foreign affairs. Demands for autonomy or "self-determination" can range from modest campaigns for linguistic rights to calls for outright self-rule within a federal or loose confederal structure, or even a separate and sovereign state. Campaigns for secession are more likely to develop when previously acquired privileges are under threat or when underprivileged groups seize an opportunity to redress their grievances and push for separate statehood.

A central problem in Eastern Europe revolves around the distinction between "civil rights" (which belong equally to all individuals) and "group rights." Not all administrations that guarantee the former necessarily recognize the latter. Officials may fear that bestowing special privileges or implementing "affirmative action" programs for minorities may worsen ethnic relations by breeding resentment among the majority while arousing unacceptable minority aspirations for autonomy. Ethnic conflicts tend to intensify in states that either fail to ensure minority protection or inhibit the emergence of a nonethnic civil society based on social mobility and occupational opportunity. In the latter instance, national identity and full citizenship rights may become the exclusive province of a single ethnic group.

Since the anticommunist revolutions of 1989, a plethora of ethnically exclusive associations have sprung to life in each East European state, representing both majority and minority groups. While some organizations remain principally concerned with cultural, linguistic, educational, and religious rejuvenation, others have pressed for wide-ranging political and economic concessions. Some of these groups have a moderate political agenda, but others have adopted more militant positions toward self-determination. While some minority organizations have been accommodated in the emerging system of political pluralism, others are viewed with suspicion and distrust. In the midst of a destabilizing period of democratic restoration, ethnic politics has begun to seem important not only to minority groups seeking greater self-determination, but also to some majorities fearful of losing influence or access to key resources.

Nationalist organizations of various hues have sprung up among the majority nationalities. Some are suspected of being fronts or proxies for the disempowered communist *apparat,* while others have been created by former anticommunist dissidents. Various competing political formations have taken up nationalist issues with a view to garnering popular support. The emergence of a traditional democratic left-to-right political spectrum has been impeded by the entangling embrace of nationalist, ethnic, and regionalist politics. Indeed, the dividing line between "civics" and "ethnics" can cut across the left-right continuum, often confusing the ideological identity of specific parties. Both a nonethnic civic orientation and a collectivist ethnic-based option have been adopted by parties espousing right-wing, centrist, or left-wing economic programs. Moreover, the focus on national and ethnic questions has often delayed the formulation of clear socioeconomic programs and identities among political parties.

Varieties of Ethnic Politics

Ethnic politics in postcommunist Eastern Europe can be divided into five major variants: cultural revivalism, political autonomism, territorial self-determinism, separatism, and irredentism. The precise form it takes depends on historical traditions, on the policies and objectives of ethnic organizations, and on the comparative position of ethnic communities within existing state structures. These five variants may not be mutually exclusive or permanent even among a single nationality represented by several competing political organizations, and in some cases they can be envisaged as potential stages of development. The programs and goals of distinct ethnic communities depend on several interrelated factors, including the response of the government to minority demands and the policies of foreign governments in sponsoring or discouraging various autonomist movements. A few examples will serve to highlight the key features of the five major variants of East European ethnic politics.

Cultural Revivalism: This phenomenon is particularly noticeable among small or dispersed ethnic, religious, or regional minorities. Despite limited experiences of sovereignty or statehood, their leaders may demand the freedom and resources to rebuild their social, cultural, religious, and educational institutions; to redefine their history; to reinforce their identity; and to revive their dialect or language. These objectives may be framed in the context of increasing minority participation in regional and national politics rather than as a challenge to the integrity of the state. For example, a comprehensive cultural revival has been visible among the Romany (Gypsy) population throughout Eastern Europe, a group that continues to be subject to widespread prejudice and discrimination.

Such goals have also been visible among the Ukrainians and Ruthenians in Poland and Slovakia. The Ukrainian-Ruthenian ethnic group in Poland numbers about 300,000 people scattered throughout the country, the most substantial minority in ethnically homogeneous Poland (see Table 2). Following the democratic changes of 1989, a Union of Ukrainians in Poland (UUP) was established to defend minority rights in culture, education, language, and religious life. These activities won approval among officials in Warsaw. But more contentious issues also materialized, including calls for the return of Ukrainians to the Bieszczady Mountains (from which thousands had been deported after World War II on charges of collaboration with anticommunist guerrillas), and the return of property seized by the state in the late 1940s.

An additional complication has arisen in that many "Ukrainians" consider themselves to be "Lemko" Ruthenians (so called from a word that is unique to their local dialect). Indeed, since the collapse of communism a revival of Ruthenian consciousness has been visible throughout the Carpathian region of Central Europe. Local intellectuals have condemned centuries of assimilation attempts by neighboring Slavic nations and sought to reconstruct and develop their Ruthenian heritage, linguistically, culturally, and eventually politically. Lemko leaders in Poland, who estimate their community's numbers at around 80,000, have established citizens' circles to press for their rights as a distinct ethnic and cultural minority. Conflicts have persisted over the precise ethnic affiliation of the Lemkos and whether they form a separate nationality or are part of a larger Ukrainian nation. Some younger Polish Lemkos have adopted more militant positions, even refusing to cooperate with

Table 2 — Significant Minorities in Eastern Europe

COUNTRY	NUMBER	% of POPULATION	COUNTRY	NUMBER	% of POPULATION
Albania			*Montenegro*		
Greeks	58,758	1.85	Muslims	89,932	14.62
Bosnia-Herzegovina			Serbs	57,176	9.29
Muslims	1,902,954	43.60	Albanians	40,880	6.64
Serbs	1,370,476	31.40	*Poland*		
Croats	755,071	17.30	Ukrainians-Ruthenians	315,000	0.81
Bulgaria			Belarusans	200,000	0.52
Turks	822,253	9.70	*Romania*		
Romanies (Gypsies)	287,732	3.40	Hungarians	1,620,199	7.12
Pomaks	65,546	0.77	Romanies (Gypsies)	409,723	1.80
Croatia			Germans	119,436	0.52
Serbs	581,663	12.16	*Serbia*		
Muslims	43,469	0.91	Albanians	1,727,541	16.70
Czech Republic			Montenegrins	520,508	5.03
Moravians	1,359,432	13.20	Hungarians	345,376	3.34
Slovaks	308,962	3.00	Muslims	327,390	3.16
Hungary			Romanies (Gypsies)	137,265	1.33
Romanies (Gypsies)	404,461	3.90	Croats	115,463	1.12
Germans	175,000	1.69	*Slovakia*		
Slovaks	110,000	1.06	Hungarians	566,741	10.76
Macedonia			Romanies (Gypsies)	80,627	1.53
Albanians	427,313	21.01	Czechs	53,422	1.01
Turks	97,416	4.79	Ukrainians-Ruthenians	30,784	0.58
Romanies (Gypsies)	55,575	2.73	*Slovenia*		
Serbs	44,159	2.17	Croats	54,212	2.76
			Serbs	47,911	2.44
			Muslims	26,842	1.37

All figures are based on official censuses and estimates.

the Union of Ukrainians. Nevertheless, the Lemko organizations are not separatist and they support Poland's territorial integrity. Their chief objectives are the restoration of Ruthenian cultural rights and the expansion of Lemko educational institutions.

According to official estimates some 30,000 Ruthenians and Ukrainians live in eastern Slovakia, although unofficial calculations place the figure at over 100,000. Their official organization, the Union of Ukrainians and Ruthenians in Czechoslovakia (UURCS), supported the preservation of the Czech and Slovak Federative Republic (CSFR) and criticized the successful efforts of Slovak parties to create an independent Slovak republic. The UURCS feared that the rights of various minorities in Slovakia might be denied when Prague was no longer in a position to protect their interests. In the 1991 census of the CSFR, a Ruthenian nationality was registered for the first time without parentheses, and almost half of those who had previously declared themselves Ukrainian opted to be known as Ruthenian instead. Slovakian Ruthenians have become more active through the social-cultural organization Ruthenian Revival (RR), which organized the First World Congress of Ruthenians in March 1991. Congress participants also pressed for the recognition of Ruthenian cultural and educational organizations in Ukraine, but demanded neither autonomy nor self-determination. The Ruthenian language has been in the process of codification, to distinguish it from both Slovak and Ukrainian, and Ruthenian cultural traditions are being cultivated to help develop a distinct ethnic identity. Some extremist elements based in neighboring Ukraine have issued more far-reaching demands for Ruthenian self-government, but do not seem to have elicited much of a response in Slovakia.

Political Autonomism: This type of politics is characterized by a more pronounced form of self-organization among minority groups who have constituted majorities in previously existing states, who possess a history of organized political involvement in a multiethnic country, or whose ethnic compatriots currently constitute the majority nationality in a neighboring state. Examples of such movements are found among the Hungarians in Slovakia and the Romanian region of Transylvania. Calls for political autonomy rather than territorial self-government are more likely in ethnically mixed regions where no single group predominates and where the regime permits the active participation of minorities in political life.

The Hungarian minority in Slovakia numbers nearly 570,000, totalling almost 11 percent of the population. In some southern Slovak counties, Hungarians comprise about half of the inhabitants. After the democratic revolution in November 1989, Hungarian activists began to organize openly and to campaign for minority rights. Three main associations were formed: the Independent Hungarian Initiative (IHI), the Hungarian Christian Democratic Movement (HCDM), and the Forum of Hungarians in Czechoslovakia (FHC). The Forum later renamed itself Coexistence (Együttélés) and endeavored to involve other minorities (Poles, Ruthenians, Ukrainians) in a common front to promote minority interests. Whereas the IHI declared that campaigns for minority rights should not take precedence over the broader democratization process, Coexistence viewed the nationality issue as paramount and was criticized for being too radical and nationalistic. This did not deter

"Hungarian activists remained fearful of growing ethnic chauvinism in the independent Slovak state....."

its leaders, who denied that they were seeking territorial autonomy or secession from Slovakia. Their program called for equitable representation for Hungarians and other minorities in state institutions as well as the protection of cultural, educational, and religious freedoms. Coexistence stood on a combined list with the HCDM in the June 1990 general elections and won 14 percent of the vote, thereby gaining 14 seats in the 150-member Slovak National Council. In the June 1992 elections, it retained the same number of seats.

Coexistence has demanded the banning of various forms of official discrimination against the Magyar-speaking population, in addition to minority participation in public administration. It protested the Slovak government's mid-1991 decision to cut subsidies to minority cultural organizations, and called for the expansion of Hungarian educational, publishing, and media activities. Hungarian groups insisted that the position of minorities was under threat from rising Slovak nationalism. For instance, Coexistence objected to the package of language laws introduced by Bratislava in October 1990 that made Slovak the chief official language even in minority areas. Instead, Coexistence proposed legislation allowing the public use of minority languages in all areas with significant minorities, and not just in districts with at least 20-percent minority populations. Hungarian activists remained fearful of growing ethnic chauvinism in the independent Slovak state that emerged with the dissolution of the CSFR on New Year's Day 1993. At its fourth congress in February 1993, Coexistence condemned what it considered repressive government policies and advocated "political and economic self-administration" for the Hungarian-populated areas of southern Slovakia.

Over one and a half million Hungarians reside in Romania, constituting about 7 percent of the total population. The majority live in fairly compact areas in Transylvania, where they once benefited from substantial autonomy. The repressive policies of communist dictator Nicolae Ceauşescu were calculated to undermine Hungarian identity by restricting the media exposure and public use of the Magyar language, shrinking the Magyar educational system, and minimizing contacts across the Transylvanian-Hungarian border. During the 1980s, Ceauşescu launched a forced village-resettlement program that was intended to destroy Hungarian cultural traditions and homogenize the population. The program was abandoned after Ceauşescu was toppled from power and executed in December 1989, and the Hungarian minority then began to organize and campaign for its human rights and cultural freedoms.

Both Hungarians and Romanians participated in the demonstrations that contributed to Ceauşescu's fall. Soon afterwards, Hungarians gained the right to establish their own organizations, and in early 1990 the Democratic Alliance of Hungarians in Romania (DAHR) was formed. It claimed 200,000 members, making it the largest Magyar organization in the country. The DAHR did not call for the secession of Transylvania, but spoke out for the protection of Magyar cultural, educational, linguistic, economic, and political liberties, taking part in both the 1990 and 1992 general elections and becoming the second-strongest party in the country. DAHR leaders complained that the authorities in Bucharest had failed to guarantee the "collective national rights" of ethnic minorities, including the right to use the Hungarian language, the restoration of the Magyar educational system, proportional representation at all administrative levels, and the creation of a ministry for nationality affairs. Even though the position of minorities substantially improved, many of the gains seemed to lack firm legal safeguards to lock them in place. DAHR leaders expressed concern over a number of provisions in Romania's constitution, including its definition of the country as a "unitary national state" and the outlawing of activities falling under the vague rubric of "separatism." These leaders also feared the possibility of plans to make Romanian the exclusive official language, and to ban ethnic parties. Their fears were exacerbated after the February 1992 local elections and the September 1992 general elections, when Romanian ultranationalist parties captured over 10 percent of the vote and won several mayoral races, including the one in the Transylvanian city of Cluj-Napoca.

The declared long-term aim of the Hungarian-speakers in Romania is a guarantee of "autonomous self-administrative rights," but there are no evident intentions of forcing border changes to return any Transylvanian territories to Hungary. Hungarian political leaders in Romania have proposed extensive administrative decentralization in minority areas, allowing bilingualism to prevail in official dealings and making local self-government far more representative than it now is. DAHR leaders oppose "territorial autonomy" (in contrast to cultural and political autonomy) because Hungarian communities in mixed areas would be left outside the "autonomous region" and would be unable to benefit from "group rights." At the Third Congress of the DAHR in January 1993, moderation prevailed; nonetheless, the Association reiterated its calls for "communitarian autonomy" for the Hungarian population, and signaled that an escalation of Romanian nationalism could provoke increasing Magyar militancy.

Territorial Self-Determinism: This goal is visible among large, well-organized, and territorially compact ethnic or subethnic groups in districts where they form a relative or absolute majority of the population. Ethnic leaders may seek to reorganize the administration of the state from a unitary to a federal or confederal structure in which specific regions gain some degree of provincial autonomy or full republican status. In recent years a movement of this kind has emerged in Moravia, one of the two principal historic regions (the other is Bohemia) of the Czech Republic.

Although most Moravians consider themselves part of the Czech nation, since the Velvet Revolution of 1989 the question of Moravian-Silesian regional identity has gained increasing prominence, with some activists even seeking to resuscitate memories of the early-medieval Greater Moravian Empire. In January 1991, several newly formed Moravian groups published a "Charter for Moravia and Silesia" and called for the creation of a Moravian-Silesian parliament, the redrawing of the region's historic boundaries and electoral districts, and a reallocation of resources designed to give the region more control over its own economic affairs. In the June 1990 elections, the Movement for Self-Governing Democracy for Moravia and Silesia (MSDMS) won more than 10 percent of the vote (giving it 22 seats in the Czech National Council) and placed demands for regional autonomy firmly on the political agenda. In the March 1991 census, nearly half of the region's three million people openly declared their nationality as Moravian or Silesian for the first time in recent history. In February 1991, deputies from an assortment of Moravian parties demanded that the Czechoslovak federal authorities work out a constitutional variant for a tripartite federation and proposed the drafting of a separate Moravian constitution.

The Slovak drive for independence has also had an impact in Moravia, encouraging some activists to demand extensive decentralization of the Czech Republic. Moravian leaders began preparations for a Moravian-Silesian constitution while seeking roundtable talks with the Czech government. While some activists demanded republican status in a tripartite federation, others proposed creating two autonomous regions within the Czech Republic—Bohemia and Moravia-Silesia. In March 1991, representatives from 25 Moravian movements rejected a draft of the federal constitution because it did not accord the region federal status equal to that of the Czech Republic and

Slovakia. At a founding meeting in November 1991, the newly formed
Moravian-Silesian Council (MSC), comprising 13 organizations, called
for an equal and sovereign status for Moravia-Silesia in a Czech
federation. Some more radical groups also appeared, calling for full
Moravian sovereignty. According to public opinion polls, support for
Moravian self-determination and republican status has increased during
the past few years, even though the MSDMS won only 14 seats in the
Czech National Council in the June 1992 elections.

Separatism: This political tendency characteristically manifests itself
among ethnically and territorially compact populations, usually with
some history of statehood, who oppose any form of inclusion in the
existing federal or unitary state in which they find themselves living,
and campaign to create their own independent state structures. In recent
years, such movements have included the Slovenes and Croats in the
former Yugoslavia.

Slovenia was the westernmost and most ethnically homogeneous
republic in the Yugoslav state, with Slovenes comprising 90 percent of
the population, and was not embroiled in territorial or minority conflicts
with neighbors. The republican elections in 1990 were won by the
proindependence coalition DEMOS (Democratic Opposition of Slovenia).
In July 1990, the National Assembly adopted a proclamation on the
republic's sovereignty and prepared a constitution that would supersede
all Yugoslav federal laws. In December 1990, proindependence forces
overwhelmingly won a plebiscite on the issue, further aggravating
Slovenia's dispute with the federal authorities. Slovene leaders in the
capital of Ljubljana sought a loose confederal arrangement with other
republics, but made it clear that if an agreement could not be reached
Slovenia would declare independence. In February 1991, the National
Assembly annulled all federal laws and Slovenian obligations to
Belgrade and set a four-month deadline for independence if efforts to
form a confederation collapsed.

Immediately after Slovenia's declaration of independence, the Serb-led
federal army mounted an armed intervention to disarm the republic's
defense forces and gain control over its frontiers. The Serb generals
wanted to show that Slovenia did not qualify as an independent state
because its government did not control the republic's territory. But
Yugoslav commanders seriously miscalculated: their incursion stiffened
Slovenian resistance and united all the republic's political forces in a
common front against the invaders. Ljubljana's defense units proved
sufficiently well-organized to resist the assault, and the highly motivated
Slovene militiamen gave the federal army a bloody nose. Yugoslav and
Slovenian authorities signed the EC-sponsored Brioni cease-fire
agreement in July 1991. Slovenia and Croatia suspended their
declarations of independence for three months, pending new

interrepublican negotiations. During the moratorium, federal forces withdrew most of their contingents from Slovenia. When talks on confederation finally collapsed, Slovenia successfully reasserted its full independence from Yugoslavia.

In the republican elections of April 1990, Croatia elected a right-of-center proindependence government based around the Croatian Democratic Union (CDU), whose leader Franjo Tudjman became president. Serbia reelected an authoritarian and profederalist administration under the presidency of Serbian Socialist Party (SSP) leader Slobodan Milošević. Croatia sought a much looser confederal association, while the Serbian authorities were determined to preserve a federation in which Belgrade would remain dominant. While the secession of Slovenia appeared acceptable to Serbia, as it would strengthen Serbian demographic strength vis-à-vis the remaining republics, the separation of Croatia proved more problematic. The Milošević regime asserted that Croatia could in principle leave Yugoslavia, but could not take with it its large Serbian minority. Zagreb's secession would provoke Serbian claims to Serb-inhabited territories in Croatia and other Yugoslav republics, leading either to the establishment of a smaller Serb-dominated Yugoslavia or a so-called Greater Serbia. In June 1991, Croatia declared its independence. The Yugoslav federal army became the instrument of Milošević's program, aiming either to ensure that Zagreb remained in a centralized Yugoslavia, or else seeking to carve away some of Croatia's territory in order to build Greater Serbia.

The strategy for achieving these ends was prepared well in advance of Croatia's declaration of independence. The large Serbian community living along the border between Croatia proper and the ethnically mixed province of Bosnia-Herzegovina became a locus of guerrilla operations. Serbs constituted over 12 percent of Croatia's population, and nearly one quarter lived in the contested region, where they outnumbered Croats three-to-one. The Serb strategy was to capture and "ethnically cleanse" extensive and contiguous tracts of territory and to cut off the economically critical regions of Slavonia and Dalmatia from Zagreb. Serb guerrillas forcibly expelled Croat residents from the contested zones in order to leave Serbs in the majority. By December 1991, Serb forces had gained control of one quarter of Croatia's territory, styling this conquered tract the Republic of Serbian Krajina. At this point, UN forces were allowed to patrol the territory and freeze the occupation while Belgrade turned its attentions to hapless Bosnia-Herzegovina. Throughout 1992-93, Zagreb complained that the UN was failing to fulfill its mandate to restore Croatian authority in the occupied zones.

Irredentism: Separatist movements in one state may seek to join their territories and populations with another existing state, either as an autonomous region or as an integral administrative unit. In some instances, such movements may be directly sponsored by a neighboring state seeking to expand its own borders. Pertinent examples of separatist-irredentists include the Serbs in both Croatia and Bosnia-Herzegovina and the Croats in the latter province.

Of the approximately 4.2 million residents of Bosnia-Herzegovina, Muslims accounted for about 44 percent, Serbs 31 percent, and Croats 17 percent. With Slovenia and Croatia pushing toward secession in 1990-91, leaders of Bosnia's chief ethnic groups found themselves under great pressure to side with either Serbia or Croatia. Serb authorities in Belgrade and Bosnian Serb leaders began to worry about the prospect of a Muslim-Croat majority coalition in Bosnia that could shut Serbs out of power within the province and form ties to Croatia. Meanwhile, Muslims and Croats grew concerned that Serbian minority leaders in league with the Milošević regime were planning to foment a crisis similar to the one that had left Croatia stripped of a quarter of its land and with several of its cities reduced to rubble.

The year-old Yugoslav war and its horrors spread to Bosnia-Herzegovina in April 1992. The Belgrade regime helped to launch a new land-grabbing operation on the pretext that Serbs had a right to "self-determination" and did not recognize existing republican borders. Bosnian Serb irregulars and Yugoslav army units, supplemented by troops shifted from the now-quiet Croatian front and by nationalist guerrillas infiltrated from Serbia and Montenegro, began a major offensive across Bosnia. The objective was to expand those territorial enclaves controlled by Serbs who refused to recognize the authority of the Sarajevo government or the legality of Bosnia's March 1992 declaration of independence. The operational plan involved linking up five previously declared "autonomous republics" by forcibly expelling Muslims and Croats from municipalities in which Serbs formed relative minorities.

With overwhelming firepower and Belgrade's covert backing, Serb forces rapidly gained control of nearly 70 percent of Bosnia's territory. Bosnian government troops were caught unprepared and suffered serious casualties across the republic. Serbian "ethnic cleansing" techniques, first used on Croatian territory the previous year, were applied across Bosnia. By early 1993, over a million refugees had been expelled from their homes in this monstrous campaign and over 120,000 people had reportedly perished. Ethnic conflicts were manufactured across Bosnia by radical politicians (especially on the Serb side) as smokescreens for their strategic objectives. Meanwhile, Serb leaders in Belgrade proclaimed a third Yugoslavia. They adopted a new constitution that left open the possibility of other self-declared "Serbian" states in Croatia and Bosnia joining the new federation.

As the war escalated, Croatian authorities in Herzegovina formed their own army and administration while pledging allegiance to the Muslim-led regime in Sarajevo. In July 1992, the Croatian Defense Council declared the autonomy of the "Community of Herzeg-Bosnia" with its capital in Mostar. The move heightened speculation that Zagreb was negotiating a secret partition agreement with Serb leaders. Croat spokesmen contended that "Herzeg-Bosnia" was only a temporary arrangement to assure administrative continuity in wartime conditions. But suspicions remained that as Bosnia splintered, Croatia would claim its share of about a fifth of the republic, particularly those municipalities in Herzegovina where Croats formed absolute majorities. Throughout early 1993, the UN pressed the three sides to accept the Vance-Owen Plan for cantonizing Bosnia. When the plan collapsed in the spring of 1993—principally because of Serb opposition to the proposed territorial divisions requiring the surrender of a quarter of Serb-held land—the partitioning of Bosnia accelerated. Serbs and Croats increasingly collaborated in consolidating their quasi-state units in preparation for merger with their "mother" republics, leaving a Muslim-dominated rump state in the center of what was once Bosnia-Herzegovina.

Ethnic Ethics

To prevent ethnic relations in various parts of Eastern Europe from spiralling out of control and provoking the kind of violence witnessed in the Yugoslav successor states, international organizations should join the states and ethnic minorities of the region in enacting a timely series of measures. Incumbent governments desirous of political legitimacy and economic assistance must act swiftly to ensure the full array of internationally sanctioned minority rights in national constitutions and other legal documents. These include guarantees of nondiscrimination on ethnic, religious, or racial grounds, as well as the opportunity to express and develop minority cultures and languages. Even if the state cannot provide separate or supplemental schooling and other resources, it should give minorities maximum leeway to establish and control their own private educational and cultural institutions. Furthermore, minorities must be allowed to participate fully in the country's political system through involvement in national and local elections. It would be difficult to dictate the precise form of minority representation, whether this is based on ethnic proportionality or regulated quotas at local, regional, and national levels. But agreements must be reached that on the one hand satisfy minority aspirations, and on the other hand reassure majorities that their rights will not suffer as a consequence. Indeed, an absence of such provisions and the exclusion of minorities from the formulation and administration of laws will do nothing but heighten calls for political self-determination and separatism.

Minority leaders must also abide by specific obligations to the state. Principally, they have to affirm its legitimacy and territorial integrity when minority interests are reasonably respected and represented, regardless of the precise administrative structure. Indeed, they will have sounder justifications for opposition and autonomy in a nondemocratic polity than in a country that guarantees fundamental individual and group rights. In cases of the former sort, they will also have recourse to international intervention and mediation as a means to pressure the government to enshrine minority rights in appropriate legal documents. Although such measures will not eliminate all the wellsprings and occasions of conflict, they can provide a basis for dialogue and compromise.

The international arena is equally important for ensuring that states and minorities can interact peacefully and productively. Each government needs to conclude bilateral agreements with neighbors, mutually guaranteeing the rights of resident minorities and renouncing any territorial pretensions. If need be, a binational or multinational monitoring group could be established to report on the position of minorities in both states. Beyond this, the Conference on Security and Cooperation in Europe (CSCE), with its newly appointed High Commissioner of National Minorities, and other international organizations could take steps toward forging a charter that would codify minority rights everywhere in Europe. This international agreement would help clarify the obligations of both states and their constituent minorities. Such a document would receive powerful practical reinforcement from the creation of a committee of international legal experts and observers who can be promptly dispatched to monitor the observance of charter provisions, provide early warnings of conflict, issue recommendations for countermeasures, and help to provide a needed forum for the mediation of disputes.

Continuing calls for neutrality over the question of minority or group rights and an exclusive focus on individual human rights simply sidestep a problem that will bedevil Eastern Europe for at least the next decade. Indeed, neglecting the issue may have an opposite effect from the one intended, giving governments the go-ahead to pursue assimilation and undermine the identity of distinctive ethnic, cultural, and religious minorities. This, in turn, could provoke conflicts between neighboring states and threaten regional stability. By contrast, the early and consistent involvement of international institutions in improving ethnic relations could directly assist the democratization process, help to move each country toward observance of accepted international standards, and militate against ethnic polarization and its attendant dangers.

8.
SERBIA'S ROAD TO WAR

V.P. Gagnon, Jr.

V.P. Gagnon, Jr. is an SSRC-MacArthur Foundation Postdoctoral Fellow in Peace and Security in a Changing World. He is currently a visiting fellow at the Peace Studies Program, Cornell University, where he is working on a book about the Yugoslav crisis. He will spend the 1994-95 academic year in the former Yugoslav region.

Not so long ago, Yugoslavia was the shining star of Eastern Europe. Although it faced structural problems similar to those of the other socialist countries, it was open to Western culture, its citizens traveled and worked throughout Western Europe, its political elite was much more cosmopolitan and Western-oriented than that of other socialist countries, and concepts of liberal democracy were openly discussed and advocated within the ruling Communist party. Indeed, at a time when Mikhail Gorbachev was taking the first tentative steps in the process of change within the Soviet Union, in Yugoslavia secret-ballot multicandidate elections were being held not only within the Communist party, but also among the wider population for top state officials. Within the ruling party itself, arguments were being made about the necessity of multiparty democracy and of private property as the "pillar of the economy." Although the Yugoslav federation clearly faced some restructuring and political conflict, it was far ahead of the curve compared to other socialist countries in the region.

In the forefront of these liberal trends was Serbia's Communist party and much of the Serbian intelligentsia centered in Belgrade. Democratic currents were also strong in Slovenia and existed in every Yugoslav republic's communist party to some extent. Yet Serbia's centrality as the largest republic, the Serbs' status as the largest nationality group in Yugoslavia, and Belgrade's dual status as both the federal and the Serbian capital made Serbia's liberals extremely well-placed to guide the country toward pluralism.

Since the spring of 1991, however, Yugoslavia has been consumed by a cruel, multisided war that has left hundreds of thousands dead, turned millions more into refugees, and horrified the entire world. Although often explained and even justified in terms of ethnicity and the historical and cultural legacies of the Balkans, the war has in fact been part of a purposeful and rational strategy planned and carried out by the minority of political actors in Serbia who were most threatened by democratizing and liberalizing currents within the Serbian Communist party. Far from being the spontaneous eruption of "ancient ethnic hatreds" brewing in a cultural and historical context hostile to democratization, or the natural result of some objective conflict of interest between ethnic groups, the war was begun precisely *because* of the relative strength of homegrown pressure for political pluralism and support for liberal democratic values, especially in Serbia.

A shared desire to halt these trends brought together a coalition comprising conservatives at the top of the Serbian party, local and regional party elites whose position and power were integrally bound to the old system, old-line Marxist intellectuals, and elements of the Yugoslav Army (JNA) whose political power and material privileges were the first targets of democratic forces. This coalition used the rhetoric of ethnicity and nationalism to provoke violent conflict along ethnic lines—first to mobilize against Serbian party reformists and to take control of the Serbian and other republic-level parties, and then to prevent newly active noncommunist democratic forces in Serbia from mobilizing the wider population against the regime. The original goal was to recentralize the Yugoslav federation under a newly monolithic and hard-line Communist party. When the revolutionary events of 1989-90 in Eastern Europe and a backlash against Serbian policies in other Yugoslav republics made this objective unattainable, Serbian conservatives moved to destroy Tito's Yugoslavia and to build on its ashes a "Greater Serbia" in which they could continue to use an image of threatened Serbdom to slow or halt the shift toward pluralism sweeping the region. This strategy not only severely weakened the democratically inclined opposition within Serbia, but also bolstered antidemocratic forces in the other republics, particularly Croatia. Conflict along ethnic lines was thus actively created and provoked by certain political actors in order to forestall native trends toward democratization.

The conventional wisdom about Yugoslavia's ordeal is that democratization was impossible because of the supposedly ancient ethnic hatreds that burst forth as soon as communist rule ended and that doomed the region to nightmarish violence. Ethnic conflict is thus taken as natural and inevitable, and all analyses flow from that "fact."

Yet arguments focusing on ancient hatreds as the main cause of the conflict are highly misleading. As specialists in the study of ethnic conflict have pointed out, "history can be a weapon, and tradition can fuel ethnic conflict, but a current conflict cannot generally be explained by simply calling it a revived form of an earlier conflict."[1] Interethnic relations in Yugoslavia, moreover, were not especially bitter. One very telling piece of evidence is the high rate of intermarriage in the most ethnically mixed parts of Croatia and Bosnia; sociologists and scholars of ethnicity recognize this as a key indicator of social integration and minimal antagonisms along ethnic lines.[2] This is not to say, of course, that there were no disagreements or conflicting claims between Yugoslav republics or those who claimed to speak on behalf of ethnic groups. But it is clear that such tensions were by no means fated to lead to the awful bloodshed that we have been witnessing.

In fact, the conflict did not erupt on its own in these ethnically mixed regions. There was no spontaneous resurgence of submerged or repressed "ethnic hatreds," but rather a purposeful and active creation and exploitation of such hatred as a means of stopping or slowing shifts in the locus and structure of power in Serbia. To understand how the hard-liners' coalition in Serbia managed this feat, we must cast our glance backward at what has happened in Yugoslavia over the last three decades.

Reformists versus Conservatives

Conservative forces in Serbia first began trying to exploit ethnic conflict and threatening images of the ethnic other at the onset of the first real period of liberalization in Yugoslavia, in the mid-1960s. Faced with declining economic performance and realizing the need to shift from extensive to intensive forms of economic growth, liberals in the communist leadership convinced Tito of the absolute necessity of decentralizing the economy and political system. These leaders openly questioned the most basic concepts of Marxism-Leninism and sought, as one of them put it, "to bring Europe into Yugoslavia." These policies were very popular both within the party and among the wider population. The young liberal party leaderships of Serbia, Croatia, and other republics mobilized this wider popularity against their conservative opponents, making the latter feel threatened indeed.

A few conservative bureaucrats and intellectuals in Serbia sought to discredit the reforms by denouncing them as anti-Serb and linking them to the "historical enemies" of Serbia. Despite the removal of these outspoken conservatives from the party in 1968, by 1971 the growing popularity of the reformist leaders and the increasing threat that their policies posed to the very bases of conservative power led desperate hard-liners in the Serbian party and the federal armed forces to compare the reform movement with the Croatian fascist Ustaše party of World War II. Although the reforms were far from promoting counterrevolution or fascism, conservative denunciations of the threat of "Croatian nationalism" succeeded in dividing the reformist forces in Yugoslavia.

Federal tanks rolled into the streets of Zagreb, the Croatian party's leadership was removed from power, and reformists were purged. A year later the popular Serbian reformist leadership suffered a similar fate, as did reformists in the other Yugoslav republics.

One of the results of this conservative victory was a deepening of the economic crisis in the late 1970s. To prepare for the inevitable struggle over reform that would break out after Tito's death, conservatives within the army purged reform-minded officers. At this time Slobodan Milošević, an executive of a large energy firm and an ideological conservative since joining the party at the age of 17, was elected to a top body within the army's party organization. Within Serbia, officially sponsored portrayals of Serbia as an innocent victim of the outside world began to proliferate.

Tito's death in May 1980 did indeed mark the start of an intense controversy over the future of the Yugoslav political and economic system. Since the economic situation was much worse than it had been 20 years earlier, the reformists' proposals were much more radical and attracted much broader support. In the forefront of the reformist movement were liberals within the Serbian party leadership, who called for the elimination of party bureaucrats' control over local decision making; greater reliance on private enterprise and individual initiative; multiple candidates in state and party elections; free, secret-ballot elections within the party; and the adoption of "all the positive achievements of bourgeois civilization"—i.e., liberal democratic values. By 1985, reformists were becoming dominant in the Serbian party's upper levels, and appeals were heard for the recognition of private enterprise as the "pillar of the economy," and even for a multiparty system.

Clearly, such a radical transformation threatened to destroy the ideological and institutional bases on which the conservatives' power depended. In response, conservative forces in Serbia, following the same strategy used against the reformers of the 1960s, once again cited threats to the Serbian people. This time, they began with the alleged danger posed by neighboring Albania, in particular the "Albanian menace" that threatened the very heart of the medieval Serbian kingdom, the southern province of Kosovo. By 1981, the population of this province (which had gained de facto republic status in 1974) was 75 percent ethnic Albanian, and Serbian party cadres, who had carried out very repressive policies against Kosovan Albanians prior to the 1965 reforms, had been replaced by ethnic Albanians. In the late 1970s Serbian party conservatives, supported by these embittered Kosovan Serbs, began attacking Kosovo's autonomy in an attempt to recentralize the Republic of Serbia and thereby increase Serb influence within the Yugoslav federation. Although Kosovan Serbs had legitimate grievances, the conservatives were seeking to inflame and exploit rather than resolve them. Faced with the possibility that moderate forces in the Kosovan and Serbian parties would forge a peaceful settlement of the province's status, these conservatives stepped up their rhetoric, denouncing "Albanian nationalism" and demanding a response to alleged anti-Serb "genocide" in the province.

By 1986, the Kosovo question had become the centerpiece of the conservative counterattack against the increasingly popular and successful reformists within Serbia. Under party chief Slobodan Milošević, the conservatives organized massive marches by Kosovan Serbs on Belgrade in order to discredit and marginalize the Serbian reformists (as well as reformists in the federal party) as traitors to Serbdom. This "populist" mobilization was supplemented by the actions of certain intellectuals who repeated the charge of "genocide" in a draft memorandum of the Serbian Academy of Arts and Sciences on the future of Yugoslavia. While cloaked in the rhetoric of "democracy," this document idealized the more centralized, statist, and repressive socialist system that existed in the two decades prior to 1965, and portrayed the Serb nation as living under a threat to its very existence posed by the reforms of the 1960s. It thus explicitly sought to discredit market-based economic reform and liberalizing political reform alike as "anti-Serbian."

This counterattack succeeded in staving off reformist dominance within the Serbian party by diverting attention from economic policy. The center of the party's official line now became the threat to Serbs in Kosovo rather than reform. The conservatives effectively mobilized an anti-reform coalition comprising those parts of the party and wider population who stood to lose the most from reform, especially workers in inefficient state companies, pensioners, and Serbs from underdeveloped regions. In September 1987, Milošević managed to purge reformists from the party leadership by accusing them of being "soft" on Albanians. Their crime had been to advocate a moderate, negotiated solution based on democratic principles, to warn against demonizing all ethnic Albanians, and to criticize the chauvinistic Serbian nationalism being used by conservatives. After this purge came the reimposition of a monolithic Stalinist notion of the party, a takeover of the once independent and liberal Serbian press, an extremely crude and racist campaign of demonization against ethnic Albanians, and harsh repression within Kosovo. In fact, this episode proved to be a preview of the Serbian conservatives' strategy toward the rest of Yugoslavia.

The Federal Party under Siege

Control of the Serbian party was, however, only the conservatives' first step toward ensuring their survival in power. Since each of Yugoslavia's six republics and two autonomous provinces had a vote in federal state and party organs, control of Serbia alone was not enough.

The Serbian conservatives needed to remove the danger of being outvoted by reformists in other republics, as well as prevent the possibility of federal-level alliances between Serbian reformists and their counterparts in other republics. Milošević thus quickly moved to take over other republics' party leaderships. He was successful in Vojvodina and Montenegro (both of which have large Serb populations), where his supporters used the same strategy of mob rallies and appeals to threatened Serbdom. But this strategy backfired in the other republics. Publication in May 1988 of army plans to arrest hundreds of Slovenian political and cultural figures and to use force to crush protests in Slovenia, where calls for a democratic system had gone furthest, radicalized both the party and the people at large in that republic. By mid-1988, there had been an unofficial referendum on Slovenian independence, and the Slovenian communist party was advocating the introduction of a multiparty system. During that same year, Milošević and the JNA began to mobilize Serbs in the underdeveloped region of Croatia known as Krajina as a means of pressuring the Croatian party leadership. But these moves backfired, discrediting Croatian conservatives and thereby emboldening the reformist minority—a striking effect, given that after 1971 the Croatian party had become one of the most conservative in Yugoslavia.

At the federal level too, the conservatives faced reformist dangers. The fall of 1988 saw an unsuccessful attempt by Milošević to take over the presidency of the federal party (the League of Communists of Yugoslavia, or LCY); indeed, the LCY's central committee voted to unseat the one member of that body who was clearly Milošević's man. By March 1989, reformist forces had successfully raised to the federal premiership Ante Marković, who was committed to strengthening the federal government in order to impose market-based economic reforms and a pluralistic political system. His economic policies soon showed positive results, cutting inflation, attracting foreign investment, and reviving economic growth. He enjoyed much support within Serbia—a May 1990 poll in the newspaper *Borba* showed that Serbs gave Marković a 61-percent approval rating (compared to 50 percent for Milošević). By the end of 1989, moreover, reform communists in the Slovenian and Croatian parties had gained the upper hand by linking conservatives with Milošević's aggressive policies. In each of those two republics, multiparty elections had been scheduled for the spring of 1990. The Serbian conservatives sought to halt this trend at an extraordinary LCY congress in January 1990, but failed when the Slovenians walked out over the rejection of their demands for de jure republic party independence, the introduction of multipartyism, and human rights guarantees. The subsequent refusal of the Croatian, Bosnian, and Macedonian parties to continue the congress effectively spelled the demise of the LCY.

During this period of moves toward democratization in the northwestern republics, Serbian conservatives began a campaign to demonize Slovenes and Croats in order to prevent an alliance of Serbian reformists and democrats with similar forces in those republics. A total boycott of economic and cultural ties with Slovenia was called by the Serbian leadership, and Slovenes were denounced as "white guard" and anti-Serbian—an important first step in destroying the ties that held Yugoslavia together. At the same time, nationalist-oriented Serb intellectuals raised the specter of Croatia's wartime fascists, relying on images of massacres and mutilations of Serbian children and civilians, and none too subtly implying that Croats as a people were "genocidal." The intention was not only to demonize the Croatian people and party, but also to discredit those in the Serbian party who supported the policies of Ante Marković (a Croat).

This strategy had a paradoxical result, however, for it ensured that the spring 1990 multiparty elections in Slovenia and Croatia would be won by anticommunist nationalist parties committed (at least on paper) to a confederal Yugoslavia based on market economics and democratic principles. Indeed, even most Serbs in Croatia, especially those living in ethnically-mixed parts of the republic, rejected the overt nationalism of the Milošević-allied Serbian Democratic Party (SDS) and voted instead for the reform communists, who called for a confederal Yugoslavia and rejected Milošević's calls for greater centralization. Clearly, most of Croatia's Serbs desired above all to preserve interethnic harmony and foster prosperity, goals that they saw as better served by democracy and a free market economic system (the platform of the reformist Croatian communists) than by rule from Belgrade.

This period also saw within Serbia itself growing calls for multiparty elections, encouraged by events in the northwestern Yugoslav republics and the rest of Eastern Europe (especially the December Revolution in Romania and the execution of dictator Nicolae Ceauşescu). By the late summer of 1990, Milošević found himself forced into accepting the principle of multiparty elections.

Milošević's Strategy

In this new situation, the party membership was no longer the only group whose support was needed to maintain power. A strategy based on appeals to a xenophobic and authoritarian version of Serbian nationalism was not only insufficient to maintain power in a Yugoslavia where only 39 percent of the population was Serb, but in fact was a recipe for electoral defeat. While Milošević conceivably could have taken control of the Bosnian and even the Croatian party organizations (where Serbs were 47 and 50 percent of the party membership, respectively), he would have little chance of gaining the support of the majority of the population in those republics (where Serbs were 33 and 12 percent of the population, respectively). The electoral victory of noncommunists in Slovenia, Croatia, Bosnia, and Macedonia meant that Serbia would not be able to rule through the federal institutions, where Milošević controlled only four of the eight votes needed (those of Serbia, Kosovo, Vojvodina, and Montenegro).

Faced with this challenge to their hold on power, the Serbian conservatives and their allies in the JNA had the choice of either recentralizing the country by force of arms or destroying federal Yugoslavia and reconstructing an expanded Serbian state on its ruins. The strategy that they finally chose combined both of these approaches, and was driven by the increasing challenges posed by the democratic opposition within Serbia and among Serbs in other republics.

Finally forced to accept multiparty elections in Serbia scheduled for December 1990, and faced with anticommunist nationalist opposition parties, Milošević defended the economic achievements of socialism, while continuing his anti-Albanian rhetoric on Kosovo. The ruling party had already established itself as the "defender of Serbdom" and repudiated Tito's policy of suppressing all forms of nationalist sentiment. The Serbian conservatives also averted the emergence of a reformist social democratic party that might have more credibly appealed to people's material interests, and renamed the communist party the Socialist Party of Serbia (SPS).

In the election, the SPS argued for the continuation of the socialist system that had provided social security and economic growth, and blamed all economic problems on the "anti-Serbian" policies of Federal Prime Minister Marković. At the same time, it restricted the opposition parties' access to television, fostered a proliferation of smaller parties in order to dilute media coverage of legitimate opposition parties, and accused the anticommunist nationalist party of wanting to drag Serbia into war. While continuing its anti-Albanian posturing, it portrayed itself as moderate on the issue of interethnic relations. Finally, it used the power of the government printing press to issue US$2 billion worth of dinars for overdue worker salaries just before the elections. The SPS won an overwhelming majority of parliamentary seats in a first-past-the-post election with the support of 47 percent of the electorate.[3]

At this same time, Belgrade engineered a takeover of the Serbian party in Croatia (SDS) by hard-line forces in the underdeveloped region of Krajina, which although having a Serb majority (62 percent), contained only 30 percent of Croatia's total Serb population. Since most Croatian Serbs had indicated a preference for a moderate reformist course rather than a confrontational nationalist one, the SDS sought to provoke conflict with the Croatian government as a means of instilling fear in Croatia's Serbs. The SDS and Belgrade cited the anti-Serb campaign rhetoric of the Croatian ruling party (the Croatian Democratic

Union, or HDZ) to charge that its victory meant a return of the genocidal policies of the Ustaše. As they had in Kosovo, Serbian conservatives exploited legitimate grievances for their own ends. While Serbs in Croatia did have real concerns about the HDZ's policies, Belgrade cynically manipulated these fears. Indeed, those Serbs who sought to address their fears by negotiating with Zagreb or with Croatian opposition parties over their future status in Croatia were threatened and silenced by Milošević's allies. By August 1990, the SDS was setting up armed barricades, pressuring villages with large Serb populations to join "Krajina," and redoubling its campaign of repression against moderate Serbs.

Once Milošević's party won the December 1990 elections in Serbia, the SDS, with weapons supplied by the JNA, began provoking armed incidents with Croatian police and storming villages adjacent to Krajina. These moves spread from areas where Serbs were in the majority to areas where they were a minority. The JNA was called in to "separate" the two sides. Non-Serbs in these regions then found themselves besieged and driven from their homes. In this way, forces loyal to the Serbian conservatives began enlarging the territory under their control and "cleansing" it of non-Serbs. Belgrade characterized this conflict as "interethnic fighting," a label that the Western media unquestioningly repeated.

The Serbian Opposition

This strategy was rudely interrupted by an uprising of democratic forces within Serbia itself. In early March 1991, the democratic opposition held massive demonstrations in Belgrade, threatening to oust the ruling party by means of street rallies. The rallies were directed against the regime's tight control of broadcast media, but also condemned Milošević's economic policies and his policy of provoking conflict with other republics in the negotiations over the future of Yugoslavia (which had begun in January and in which the Serbian president had refused to budge from his demand for a more centralized federation). Milošević called in the police and army to crush the demonstrations. Although some violent means were employed, the generals refused his request to use massive force, thus compelling him to negotiate with his opponents.

The March 1991 demonstrations marked the start of a surge in the popularity of the democratic opposition parties, and the SPS felt itself rocked from within by a revolt of democratically inclined, reformist forces. Faced with these very serious challenges, Milošević accepted some opposition demands, allowed limited economic reform, and opened talks on the formation of a multiparty "Serbian national council." The government also printed more money to pay workers and quell massive strikes. In his dealings with other Yugoslav republics, Milošević also began to walk the path of compromise; in April he accepted the principle of a confederal arrangement, and in June he agreed to the basic outline of such a compromise confederation. He also pressured his Serbian allies in Croatia to resume negotiations with Zagreb.

Yet at this very same time, the Serbian regime intensified its aggressive nationalist rhetoric and purposeful incitement of ethnic conflict in Croatia. Milošević himself labeled the Serbian antiregime protesters "enemies of Serbia" who were supposedly in league with the Albanians, Croats, and Slovenes. The media increasingly portrayed the Croatian government as fascists seeking to exterminate all Serbs, and blamed Germany and Austria for supporting "Croatian fascism" in hopes of rebuilding their former empires. The SPS entered into an open alliance with the neofascist Serbian Radical Party that gave new stature to its leader, Vojislav Šešelj, who called for "ethnic cleansing" within Serbia and publicly bragged that his guerrilla groups were instrumental in the ensuing escalation of conflict in Croatia.

Within Croatia, Belgrade exerted growing pressure on moderate Serb leaders in the ethnically-mixed Slavonia region (adjacent to Serbia but where Serbs were not in the majority) to accept its confrontational policy. By May, the flow of weapons from the JNA arsenals into Krajina had dramatically increased, and Šešelj's guerrilla groups began filtering into Croatia, terrorizing Serb and non-Serb populations in Slavonia, and forcibly expelling non-Serbs from areas under its control.

In part as a response to provocations of this sort, the Croatian parliament in late June declared the start of the process of disassociation from Yugoslavia, in preparation for the new confederal agreement that had been reached earlier that month. The declaration recognized the continuing authority of federal organs, including the army, and explicitly stated that it was not an act of unilateral secession. Serbian forces nevertheless intensified and spread the war, provoking conflict in Krajina and Slavonia, terrorizing civilians, destroying non-Serb villages, and forcing Serbs to join them or die. This was a deliberate policy of violently shattering interethnic peace throughout the region. Belgrade claimed that the war was being undertaken to protect Croatia's Serbs, who were said to be threatened with "genocide," and filled the Serbian media with direct comparisons of Croatian president Franjo Tudjman and the fascist Ustaše. But outside observers such as Helsinki Watch noted that until August, when the Croats began to take the offensive, the most egregious human rights abuses were committed by the Serb irregulars and the JNA, including the destruction of entire cities by outside bombardment and the indiscriminate use of violence to terrorize Serbs into submission and to drive out non-Serbs.[4] This policy in turn provoked Croat extremists, whose own atrocities against Serbs Milošević then used as proof of Serbia's original contention.

Perhaps more important than the goals of this policy in Croatia, however, were its goals within Serbia itself. In April 1991, Serbia's democratic opposition had been at a high point: the ruling party was facing a split, and commentators were predicting the imminent fall of the SPS. But the SPS, relying on its control of the mass media, used the charges of genocide and the subsequent war in Croatia to crush internal party dissent and to marginalize the democratic opposition by drowning out concerns about reform and tarring those who questioned the war as traitors.

The regime also used the war to try to destroy the opposition physically. Reservists sent to the front were drafted first from counties that had voted for opposition parties in the elections, and opposition leaders and outspoken antiwar activists were also sent to combat zones. Any criticism of the war was met by physical threats from neofascist gangs. Many Serbs (especially young men) who opposed the war fled the country or went into hiding. The regime also targeted the Hungarian minority in Vojvodina Province (an absolute majority in seven of its counties); although Hungarians constitute only 3 percent of Serbia's population, they accounted for 7 to 8 percent of the reservists called to the front and 20 percent of casualties. In this way, the SPS was able to insulate its own core of supporters from the war's dangers and hardships.

By November 1991 the opposition was in shambles, but the domestic costs of the military strategy were growing as casualties mounted and large numbers of reservists began deserting the front due to shortages of equipment and the shortcomings of their JNA officers. The Croats were beginning to regain ground, and the European Community was preparing to recognize Croatia, thus opening the possibility of international military intervention. Such involvement seemed even more likely after Milošević's close allies in the Soviet Union—hard-liners in the army and party—failed in their attempt to take power in August 1991. By December 1991, Milošević had reversed his longstanding opposition to UN peacekeeping forces and agreed to their deployment in the Serb-occupied areas of Croatia. But even with the UN presence, terror against Serbs and non-Serbs in those areas continued.[5]

The War in Bosnia

The war in Bosnia represented a continuation of this overall strategy of provoking ethnic conflict for political ends, and followed the scenarios already enacted in Kosovo and Croatia. Indeed, though the war in Croatia had effectively erased the gains made by the opposition within Serbia in spring 1991, it also worsened the economic situation and increased overall dissatisfaction with the Milošević regime. In early 1992 the opposition therefore once again seemed on the rise, and by spring hundreds of thousands of Serbians had signed petitions calling on Milošević to resign.

It was thus no coincidence that by January 1992 the situation in Bosnia began to resemble the situation in Croatia a year earlier. The Bosnian SDS leadership had been working very closely with Belgrade since its founding in 1990 and had actively planned the war in Bosnia a year prior to its outbreak. As part of the coalition government of Bosnia, the SDS had blocked any solution to the question of the republic's future; as the war in Croatia heated up, the Bosnian SDS leadership also stepped up its anti-Muslim rhetoric. When the Croatian war wound down, the SDS in January 1992 declared an independent "Serbian Republic of Bosnia-Herzegovina" made up of majority-Serb counties that the SDS had taken over during the summer of 1991. At the same time, the SDS brutally silenced all Serb dissenters.

When Bosnian president Alija Izetbegović responded to SDS obstruction and to international recognition of Croatia by calling for a referendum on Bosnian independence, the SDS stepped up its confrontational policies, throwing up roadblocks around Sarajevo and other cities, and launched the same process of terror against Serb dissenters and ethnic cleansing against non-Serbs that was seen in Croatia. The war "officially" began on the day that Serb extremists fired on a large multiethnic peace demonstration in downtown Sarajevo, which had been the center of the Yugoslav peace movement during the Croatian conflict. By the fall of 1992, Serbian forces had consolidated their control over 70 percent of Bosnia's territory, and had forcibly expelled most of the non-Serb population.

This policy of fostering war and projecting images of threatened Serbdom has successfully prevented the mobilization of democratic opposition forces both within Serbia and among Serbs outside of Serbia. The SPS has managed to maintain its hold on power through a combination of bolstering extreme-right parties (thus making itself seem like a moderate option) and alleging an international conspiracy against innocent Serbs who are only trying to protect their homes. The limits of this policy are most clearly seen, however, at election time. In the December 1992 elections, the ruling party and its ally, the ultranationalist Radical Party, won a majority of votes only through such manipulations as tight control of television; rigging of electoral districts to favor the pro-SPS regions of central and southern Serbia; massive electoral irregularities, especially in Belgrade (where the democratic opposition was strongest); and allowing refugees from Bosnia to vote, thus bolstering the vote for the Radicals (who became the second-largest party in the Serb parliament with 29 percent of the seats, compared to 40 percent for the SPS). Another key factor was the exodus of young people and others who tended consistently to support the democratic opposition; indeed, fully a third of the Serbian electorate now consists of pensioners, Milošević's staunchest backers. Perhaps the most important factor in the SPS's success, however, has been the opposition's inability to unite, due to what the independent Belgrade weekly *Vreme* has termed "an ambivalent relation . . . to the national question." Indeed, the regime's seeming monopoly on setting the terms of political debate has led some in the democratic opposition to accept the regime's definition of Serbian national interests and to refuse to unite with those democrats who denounce the war and militarized nationalism as anathema to liberal democratic values.

This disunity of Serbia's democrats, combined with the ruling party's material and informational advantages, led to another win for the SPS in the December 1993 elections, despite a drastic deterioration in living conditions brought on by international sanctions. Motivated by the defeat of its hard-line Russian allies during the Moscow standoff in early October 1993, as well as by concern about the growing power and ambition of the Radical Party, the SPS once again tactically repositioned itself as the moderate, peace-loving party. The regime arrested a number of Radical deputies for criminal activities, and even stated its willingness to cooperate with the democratic opposition. With its iron grip on republic-wide television and its ability to cut supplies of fuel and food to the few electoral districts ruled by opposition parties (while rewarding its own supporters from reserves of food, fuel, and other goods), the SPS was able to survive another electoral challenge. In fact, the SPS significantly increased its share of the vote (although still only receiving 35 percent of the total) and added 22 seats in parliament, so it is now only three seats short of an outright majority.

Strengthening the Extremists

Its power now freshly secured at home, the regime may be even more powerfully bolstered by being allowed to carry out an internationally sanctioned annexation of those parts of Bosnia that are under its control. This "Greater Serbia" will contain the SPS's Serb-extremist allies in Bosnia—allies who were crucial in its fight against democracy within Serbia—and will have a population that is over 75 percent Serb (before the war and "ethnic cleansing," the figure for this same territory was only 45 percent Serbian). A quarter of this total Serbian population comes from economically underdeveloped regions and has been radicalized by direct suffering in the war; their presence will virtually ensure that virulent nationalist ideology will remain effective in limiting the range of legitimate political discourse. Indeed, the fact that many of the opposition parties now use the language of threatened Serbdom and defend the war signals a permanent distortion of Serbia's political climate, and means that the democratic opposition, centered in Belgrade and other cities, may be headed for permanent marginalization.

Just as disturbing—although highly desirable from the standpoint of the SPS—this policy of ethnic conflict has strengthened non-Serb extremist forces in other republics, particularly in Croatia. There, a coalition within the ruling party of former communist hard-liners (who joined the HDZ when reformists took over the Croatian communist party) and extreme authoritarian nationalists faces serious threats from HDZ moderates as well as from the increasingly popular and democratically oriented opposition party known as the Social Liberals. A key part of the conservative coalition in Croatia is made up of former hard-line communists from Herzegovina, who have taken over the Bosnian branch of the HDZ and who are using ethnic conflict in Bosnia as a way of incorporating into the Croatian electorate radicalized regional elites from underdeveloped regions of Herzegovina. (By contrast, most Bosnian Croats, who supported the now-defunct moderate wing of the Bosnian HDZ, are excluded from the Croatian-controlled ministate.) Like their counterparts in Serbia, these extremist Croats claim greater legitimacy based on their active fighting on the front lines defending innocent ethnic compatriots, and thereby try to undermine democratization.

By sanctioning a "negotiated settlement" that would divide Bosnia-Herzegovina into ethnically-pure, neo-apartheid ministates with the right to join their respective "maternal" homelands, the international community is not only betraying the ideals of liberal democracy and rewarding aggressors on all sides, but it is also strengthening the domestic positions of antidemocratic forces in Bosnia-Herzegovina, Croatia, and Serbia. Far from addressing the root causes of the strife, the West has from the beginning allowed the image of "ancient ethnic conflict" to blind it to the true nature of these wars: they are wars against *democratization* in Serbia, in Croatia, and most tragically and horrifically, in Bosnia.

NOTES

I would like to thank Jack Snyder, Val Bunce, Mark Doctoroff, and Roger Peterson for their helpful comments. I wish also to thank the SSRC-MacArthur Fellowship on Peace and Security in a Changing World and the U.S. Department of State's Title VIII Program at the Hoover Institution for funding revisions of this paper.

1. Donald Horowitz, *Ethnic Groups in Conflict* (Berkeley: University of California Press, 1985), 99. In fact, relations between Serbs and Croats in Croatia were not characterized by violent conflict before this century, and even then this was not always the case. On the history of cooperation between Serbs and Croats in Croatia, for example, see Wolfgang Kessler, *Politik, Kultur and Gesellschaft in Kroatien und Slawonien in der ersten Hälfte des 19. Jahrhunderts* (Munich: R. Oldenbourg, 1981); Sergei A. Romanenko, "National Autonomy in Russia and Austro-Hungary," in *Nationalism and Empire* (New York: St. Martin's Press, 1992); and Ljubo Boban, *Svetozar Pribićević u Opoziciji* (Zagreb: Sveučelište-Institut za hrvatsku povjest, 1973).

2. For example, the intermarriage rate of Croatia's Serbs (12 percent of the Croatian population) to Croats was consistently high throughout the 1980s (29 percent of Serbs who

married took Croat spouses). In very mixed regions of Croatia this rate was even higher, approaching 50 percent. *Demografska statistika* (Belgrade: Savezni zavod za statistiku) (annual), 1979-1989, Table 5-3. On intermarriage as an indicator, see, for example, Peter M. Blau and Joseph E. Schwartz, *Crosscutting Social Circles: Testing a Macrostructural Theory of Intergroup Relations* (Orlando, Fla.: Academic Press, 1984).

3. For a detailed description of how the SPS managed to subvert the elections and cripple the opposition, see Dušan Radulović and Nebojša Spaić, *U Potrazi za Demokratijom* (Belgrade: Dosije, 1991).

4. On the tactics used by Serbian forces, see the Helsinki Watch report "Yugoslavia: Human Rights Abuses in the Croatian Conflict," September 1991. The head of the main democratic nationalist party in Serbia, Vuk Drašković, has publicly stated that despite regime claims of "genocide" against Serbs, "there was no particular need for war in Slavonia." *Danas*, 18 February 1992; *Vreme*, 4 November 1991, 9-11. See also Helsinki Watch letter to Milošević, 21 January 1992; Blaine Harden, "Observers Accuse Yugoslav Army," *Washington Post*, 17 January 1992, A23; and Helsinki Watch, *War Crimes in Bosnia-Hercegovina* (New York, 1992).

5. See for example Helsinki Watch, *War Crimes in Bosnia-Hercegovina*, 75-81, on continued ethnic cleansing in Slavonia. The moderate Serbian Democratic Forum noted that "the level of totalitarianism in Krajina is getting higher every day, and human rights abuses are everyday events. . . . [N]ow different-minded [Serbs] are being driven into exile as well and even executed." (Ibid., 81).

9.
THE CRUEL FACE OF NATIONALISM

Vesna Pešić

Vesna Pešić *is director of the Center for Anti-War Action in Belgrade, Serbia. Active for more than two decades in movements favoring democracy and human rights, she was a founding member of the Belgrade Helsinki Committee and of the Association for a Yugoslav Democratic Initiative. Her essay is based upon remarks that she delivered at the Fourth World Conference of the National Endowment for Democracy in Washington, D.C., on 27 April 1993, on which occasion she was one of three recipients of the Endowment's biennial Democracy Award.*

With the fall of communist regimes in Europe and the demise of the bipolar structure of international relations, we are witnessing the outbreak of old conflicts and animosities among the nations and peoples of the Balkans and East Central Europe. At the same time, we are seeing the emergence of latent national and ethnic conflicts in Western Europe, as the unifying force of the Cold War and of bloc-defined politics wanes. I am convinced that the way in which the international community deals with the strife in the former Yugoslavia will have a profound impact on the resolution of Western Europe's own internal difficulties. It will also have significant repercussions for Russia and the other former Soviet republics. It would be a great tragedy if the message that is drawn from the Yugoslav crisis provides an incentive or justification for the revival of the Russian Empire or attempts to unite all Russians now living beyond the borders of the Russian Federation.

The nationalism that has recently emerged in this context is distinctly undemocratic. As such, it is reproducing the old totalitarian structures in the new postcommunist societies. In countries with historically rooted ethnic tensions and significant socioeconomic difficulties, it is introducing elements of fascism. Because of the structural similarities between communism and this brand of nationalism, it has been relatively easy to move from the one ideology to the other—that is, from one form of collectivism to the other. The former was based on class, represented by the Communist Party; the latter is founded upon ethnic homogeneity, represented by the national leader. Both systems neglect the individual and undermine the notion of rights to equal citizenship. Thus I agree with Adam Michnik, who has stated (ironically rephrasing Lenin) that nationalism is the last stage of communism. We can only hope that this stage will not last another 50 or more years.

Why is this resurgent nationalism in Eastern Europe antidemocratic? The main reason lies in the very understanding of the "nation" that forms the core of the notion of the nation-state in this region. As Julie Mostov has pointed out, membership in the nation here is defined by genealogy. That is, national identity is tied to presumed common ethnic descent as well as common language, religion, myths, and culture.[1] Citizenship rights are treated not as individual rights extended equally to all, but as the collective rights of ethnic or "national" groups. The nation is understood as a kind of superfamily. Such a conception excludes those who are not members of the dominant national group, and relegates all others to second-class citizenship.

Manipulating this kind of ethnocentric nationalism has been seen as the quickest and most effective method of gaining political power and maintaining control of the population. Old communist leaders who have recently transformed themselves into nationalists have taken this road and used national feelings and fears to serve their own ambitions. Power gained in this way is by definition authoritarian. The originally democratic idea of self-determination has become, in this context, a tool in the leaders' struggle for power.

In such struggles, particularly where armed conflicts have broken out, the use of this ethnic-based notion of nationalism has left no place for real pluralism or genuine multiparty politics. Many opposition parties have also been drawn into using nationalist appeals. Those parties or groups that have tried to withstand the pull of this force have been labeled "unpatriotic" or "traitors" and have been marginalized. Political actors have been mobilized as if they were military troops. Those who serve in parliaments are conscious that practically nothing at all is decided there. They know and implicitly accept that might will decide the direction of policy and all other matters. In this way, resistance to these nationalist regimes has been effectively undermined or destroyed.

Exclusive nationalism is expansionistic. National questions are put in terms of territorial battles to "recover" or "secure" territories in order to protect fellow nationals or national "treasures." The path of obtaining guarantees of civil and political rights for fellow nationals living beyond the boundaries of the existing nation-state is rejected in favor of resolving national questions through the occupation or annexation of territory. This leads directly to war, as well as to total control of all spheres of life—economic, social, and cultural—by the regime. Everything is subordinated to the national interest and war, which accounts for the totalitarian nature of this form of nationalism.

Why has totalitarian nationalism emerged now, in this part of the world? One reason can be traced back to the history of the Second World War. The ruling parties of some of the former communist countries (e.g., the former Yugoslavia and Soviet Union) based their legitimacy in part on their contribution to the struggle against fascism. With the fall of communism, however, the antifascist factor has largely disappeared, and latent fascist notions have thus been able to reappear in new anticommunist modes.

> *"...the war is a battle by both Serbia and Croatia to break apart Bosnia and to declare national unification with their own respective peoples on the territory of Bosnia-Herzegovina."*

Moreover, the breakdown of communist federations, as in the former Yugoslavia, has brought about the breakdown of multiethnic communities, and nationalism presents itself as a rational way to create new nation-states. As in the nineteenth century, nationalist ideology calls for the redrawing of boundaries, battles for territory, and struggles for national unification. That is why I argue that the war in Bosnia is not a civil war between three ethnic groups (indeed, grassroots ethnic conflicts rarely appeared before in this republic). Rather, the war is a battle by both Serbia and Croatia to break apart Bosnia and to declare national unification with their own respective peoples on the territory of Bosnia-Herzegovina. If you keep in mind the idea of nationally (i.e., ethnically) "pure" states, then it is clear why brutal "ethnic cleansing" is an integral element of this conflict, whose primary goal is to destroy multiethnic life.

The enormous amount of force that is needed to realize such nationally "pure" states produces authoritarian government; it also requires the large-scale development and circulation of hate propaganda. Such propaganda highlights the irrational side of nationalism, appealing to primitive emotions and making use of unprecedented attacks on others (particularly on television). The Balkans and East Central Europe offer fertile ground for this kind of propaganda because historical animosities do exist among the peoples of the region, particularly dating from the two world wars. East European countries also have felt constant tension over the insecurity of their boundaries. Because the peoples of these countries are intermingled, efforts to secure guarantees for ethnic minorities or from neighbors can pose the threat of territorial pretensions. It is easy to reignite fears that justify "defense" against aggressive aspirations to expansion and the need for protection.

The final—and perhaps the deepest—reason for the emergence of exclusive nationalism is popular fear of radical changes such as those brought about by the introduction of market economies and the opening up to the world economy. Fear of change provides a good grounding for "fundamentalist" movements—that is, movements which, in the face of uncertainty, emphasize old values such as religion, cultural and historical myths, and traditional roles and virtues. Liberalism, on the other hand, offers only uncertainty and little in the way of identity. It provides a set of "formal rules," empty roles, and an unfamiliar civic culture.

In conclusion, the war in the former Yugoslavia opens two possible paths. The first is that of war and ethnic unification; in the context of mixed communities this will only result in prolonged suffering and extensive hostilities, and further undermine the security and stability not only of the former Yugoslav republics but of the entire region and the rest of Europe as well. The second path is to establish a regional security system, mutual economic links, and social and cultural interchange that will support the development of civil states in the region and the process of European integration. It is this second option that offers our only hope for a livable future.

NOTES

1. See Julie Mostov, "Democracy and the Politics of National Identity," *Studies in East European Thought* (forthcoming, 1993).

INDEX